*Dickinson
and the
Romantic
Imagination*

Dickinson
and the
Romantic
Imagination

Joanne Feit Diehl

Princeton University Press
Princeton, New Jersey

Copyright © 1981 by Princeton University Press

Published by Princeton University Press, Princeton, New Jersey
In the United Kingdom: Princeton University Press, Guildford, Surrey

All Rights Reserved

Library of Congress Cataloging in Publication Data will be found on the last printed page of this book

This book has been composed in Linotron Bembo and Galliard

Clothbound editions of Princeton University Press books are printed on acid-free paper, and binding materials are chosen for strength and durability

Printed in the United States of America by Princeton University Press, Princeton, New Jersey

Designed by Laury A. Egan

To my Mother, Hadassah A. Feit,
and
to the memory of my Father, Charles Feit

Acknowledgments

I WISH first to thank Professor Harold Bloom, whose graduate seminar at Yale sparked my initial interest in Dickinson's relation to the Romantics. Although my current work diverges from his approach, his encouragement and continued counsel have helped form my own criticism. At a later stage, Professor Geoffrey Hartman offered advice when it was most needed. Professor Richard B. Sewall generously shared his knowledge of Dickinson and painstakingly reviewed an earlier draft of this book. I am indebted, as well, to Professor Charles Feidelson for his critical tact and attention to style.

I want to take this opportunity to thank Professor Michael J. Hoffman and the University of California, Davis, for their generous support of my work. I am grateful to the Houghton Library of Harvard University, the Sterling Library of Yale University, and the Jones Library of Amherst College for permitting me access to their Dickinson collections. My thanks to Mrs. Arthur Sherwood and Miss R. Miriam Brokaw at Princeton University Press for their patience and cooperation. Carla Lehn, with fortitude and good humor, typed, retyped, and proofread the manuscript.

I am indebted to numerous teachers, colleagues, and friends, among them Marjorie Kaufman, James McIntosh, and Thomas Woodson; Ruth Miller, M. D. Faber, and the late Laurence Holland; Catharine Stimpson, Gayatri Spivak, and Walter Reed; Max Byrd, Margaret Homans, Laura Ray, Philip E. Ray, and Elliot Gilbert.

Two friends, Ronald Sharp of Kenyon College and Evan B. Carton of the University of Texas at Austin, have, by their commitment to and interest in my work, encouraged me to clarify, as well as expand, my ideas on Dickinson.

I want especially to thank Sandra M. Gilbert, who scrutinized the manuscript in its final stages of preparation. Her

Acknowledgments

suggestions have made this a better book than it might otherwise have been; her friendship has made these final months of revision also a time of renewal. The person who, from this project's inception, has remained my most ardent critic and friend, Carl Diehl, shares in this book's dedication.

Contents

	ACKNOWLEDGMENTS	vii
	INTRODUCTION	3
I.	"Come Slowly—Eden": The Woman Poet and Her Muse	13
II.	Wordsworthian Nature and the Life Within	34
III.	Keats, Dickinson, and the Poet's Romance	68
IV.	Word and World in Shelley and Dickinson	122
V.	Emerson, Dickinson, and the Abyss	161
VI.	Afterword: On the Origins of Difference	183
	SELECTED BIBLIOGRAPHY	187
	INDEX	197
	LIST OF DICKINSON POEMS	203

*Dickinson
and the
Romantic
Imagination*

Introduction

THIS BOOK attempts a reevaluation of Emily Dickinson's poetry based upon an understanding of her relationship to the major Romantic tradition. My purpose here is not only to present a reinterpretation of Dickinson's poems, but to suggest that essential to the current reappraisal of her work is an awareness of what Dickinson shares with and how she departs from the Anglo-American Romantic tradition. The origins of this divergence are complex, but among the most important reasons is, assuredly, the fact of gender, the fact that Dickinson is a woman poet. My opening chapter, therefore, considers the implications for literary theory when the poet is a woman and, more specifically, investigates the relationship of the woman poet to her sources of "inspiration" and the tradition—to her muse. This chapter also considers the broader implications of a revisionary reading of Dickinson within and against the Romantic tradition in order to show how my interpretation of her relationship with the Romantics might apply more generally to other nineteenth-century women poets. Here I argue that Dickinson's subversion of the Romantic tradition is not an isolated phenomenon, but a process undertaken by every powerful post-Enlightenment woman poet who achieves a poetry beyond the second-rate, who frees a space for her poetic voice. After this exploratory discussion, the book turns to its central subject, an analysis of Dickinson's poetry in the context of Wordsworth, Keats, Shelley, and Emerson, an analysis which seeks to define the tradition from which Dickinson emerged as it attempts to locate her specific points of departure, the origins of her astonishingly original poetry.

Among major nineteenth-century poets, Dickinson remains the most elusive. Placed outside the development of post-Enlightenment poetry, her work is still regarded as eccentric and somehow apart, as arresting and important, but

Introduction

only tenuously related to the Romantic tradition. Can there be such a poet; can a major poet survive and grow, isolated from the central literary voices of her age? The following discussions are based upon the premise that no poet can develop in isolation from the word of his or her poetic predecessors and hope to achieve Dickinson's stature. Although a few critics, preeminently Albert Gelpi, have begun to explore instances of borrowing or thematic affinities between Dickinson and the Romantics, there has yet to appear a sustained interpretation of her poetry within the context of the Romantic tradition.[1] Only through such an interpretation, I suggest, can we begin to comprehend the experimental daring and revolutionary character of Dickinson's achievement.[2]

[1] One thinks especially of Gelpi's comments in *Emily Dickinson: The Mind of the Poet* (Cambridge: Harvard University Press, 1966), see pp. 44-45, 60, 82, 91 and *passim*; Louise Bogan's suggestions in her essay "A Mystical Poet" in *Emily Dickinson: Three Views* (Amherst: Amherst College Press, 1960) by Richard Wilbur, Louise Bogan, and Archibald MacLeish; and most directly Michael G. Yetman's "Emily Dickinson and the English Romantic Tradition" (*Texas Studies in Literature and Language*, XV. 1, Spring 1973). Yetman's brief summary of Dickinson criticism and its failure to treat her relation to the Romantics is particularly useful. To the received wisdom on Dickinson scholarship, he retorts: "Emily Dickinson did not spring full-grown from the head of Emerson, carrying a volume of Shakespeare in one hand and the King James Bible in the other, no matter how major these three sources of inspiration are to be judged in her work." (p. 130)

He continues: "A disturbing fact about much of even the most sophisticated Dickinson criticism is its reluctance to admit to significant influences on her work from outside the native tradition, almost as if to do so were to somehow weaken the poet's claim to greatness or to deter any final judgment that might otherwise be awarded her." (pp. 130-131)

[2] In other directions, Robert Weisbuch and Roland Hagenbüchle have sought to apply more sophisticated critical methods to Dickinson scholarship, and their work contributes in important ways to my study. Most significantly, these critics establish at once a clearer and more complex philosophical and linguistic context in which to place Dickinson. From another perspective, Adrienne Rich and Albert Gelpi have begun to explore the constellation of pressures and possibilities Dickinson faced as a woman poet, the relation of sexual identity to the problematics of literary creativity. Sharon Cameron, whose *Lyric Time: Dickinson and the Limits of Genre* (Baltimore and London: The Johns Hopkins University Press, 1979) appeared after the completion of my manuscript, investigates what she sees as a "cen-

Introduction

Until recently, when scholars have attempted to see Dickinson in context, most have placed her within an essentially nativist American tradition, viewing her work as seeking to resolve the tensions between Calvinist and Emersonian philosophies.³ Alternatively, critics have seen her as an isolated figure reshaping the imperial "I" of her American contemporaries into an increasingly solipsistic being. Although both observations are useful, we need not limit the context in which Dickinson worked nor deny her access to a literary tradition with which, as Richard Sewall has cogently reminded us, she was already intimately acquainted.⁴

---

tral feature of Dickinson's poetry—its resolute departure from temporal order and its reference to another absent or invisible order that is invoked as 'Immortality' or alluded to, in this case, as 'Center' " Cameron's sustained analysis of Dickinson's poetry, her investigation of the poems based upon Dickinson's desire to disrupt temporality itself, as well as Cameron's broad, generic approach—viewing Dickinson's work as a source for learning about the underlying ambitions of the lyric form—make an important addition to the field of Dickinson criticism.

³ Most critics either explicitly discuss or assume this interpretation of Dickinson's place in the tradition of American intellectual history. Among the earliest scholars to take this approach are George Frisbie Whicher and Yvor Winters (see, for example, Whicher's *This Was a Poet: Emily Dickinson* [Ann Arbor: The University of Michigan Press, 1957, originally published in 1938], p. 153 and *passim*, and Winters' "Emily Dickinson and the Limits of Judgment," originally printed in *Maule's Curse* (New Directions, 1938); reprinted in *In Defense of Reason* [Denver: Alan Swallow, 1937], p. 298). For a persuasive and thorough reevaluation of Dickinson's relation to other American writers, see Karl Keller, *The Only Kangaroo Among the Beauty: Emily Dickinson and America* (Baltimore and London: The Johns Hopkins University Press, 1979).

⁴ As Richard B. Sewall remarks in his monumental biography of Dickinson, *The Life of Emily Dickinson* (New York: Farrar, Straus and Giroux, 1974), Volume II, pp. 669-670: "She can no longer be regarded, for all her withdrawn ways, as working in grand isolation, all uniqueness and originality. She saw herself as a poet in the company of the Poets—and, functioning as she did mostly on her own, read them (among other reasons) for company."

On the implications of reading her work through the tradition, Sewall concludes: "She appears in ever-widening perspective, and her stature grows. She comes to us increasingly as the summation of a culture, not (as she was long regarded) a minor and freakish offshoot." (p. 671)

Introduction

Other critics, among them Charles Anderson and Austin Warren, emphasize the Bible as the chief external source for Dickinson's poetic strength, basing their arguments on her deep familiarity with Biblical texts, her extensive borrowing of sacred images and language, her identification of the Holy with the poetic word. As a mine for images and a resource for language, as a sublime vision of the nature of sacrifice and election, the Bible remains of central importance. Dickinson enters its lines, assumes the lives of its heroes, speaks its tongues.[5] Indeed, her use of the Bible might serve as a paradigm for her relation to other literary sources. But for Dickinson, as for other post-Miltonic poets, the Bible, though a rich source of language and meanings, is not the sole ground of struggle or single origin of the poetic *agon*. It is against human voices, as well as a sacred text, that Dickinson struggles to win her freedom.

Although the Bible contributes its vision of the Divinity of the Word, its images and language to her poetry, Dickinson

---

Extensive biographical evidence exists to justify my central assumption that Dickinson knew the English Romantics' work, as well as Emerson's, at first hand. Because my argument is not based upon the premises of a literary source study, I mention specific editions and evidence of Dickinson's reading particular poems only where appropriate throughout the text.

[5] Charles Anderson (*Emily Dickinson's Poetry: Stairway of Surprise* [New York: Holt, Rinehart and Winston, 1960]) remarks that "the gospel of St. John, one of the books she pored over, was the chief basis for uniting the symbolic meaning of the Eucharistic elements and the doctrine of the Word." (p. 42) Austin Warren asserts: "She knew her Bible well, the total Bible: it was her prime mythology." (Austin Warren, "Emily Dickinson," *Emily Dickinson: A Collection of Critical Essays*, ed. Richard B. Sewall [Englewood Cliffs: Prentice-Hall, Inc., 1963], p. 107.) In a recent essay, Vivian Pollak characterizes both the extent and nature of Dickinson's use of Biblical allusions: "The Bible, then, is the only source Dickinson exploits continuously and in depth for metaphoric allusion." And, describing the poet's relation to her source: "She is using literature most successfully as refracted imaginative experience, and she is drawn by situations which function as objective correlatives of her feelings." (Vivian R. Pollak, "Emily Dickinson's Literary Allusions," *Essays in Literature*, Western Illinois University, Volume 1, No. 1, Spring 1974, pp. 66-67.) Pollak follows in the long tradition of critics who emphasize, often to the point of excluding other influences, the importance of the Bible for Dickinson.

Introduction

turns this prepotent source toward her own concerns, which are, I will argue, the major subjects of Romanticism. Like her contemporaries Tennyson and Browning, Dickinson finds her voice in response to the controlling issues of her most powerful predecessors; and just as we cannot fully understand Tennyson and Browning without recognizing their relationship to the Romantics, so we cannot come to terms with what is most powerful in Dickinson unless we look to her forebears. We need only reexamine her poetry from this perspective to discover that her preoccupations—the self's relation to nature, the power of the imagination as it confronts death, a heroic questing that leads to a trial of the limits of poetic power—are the primary concerns of Romanticism as well.

Inevitably the subject of Dickinson's relation to the tradition leads to the more general question of the woman poet and the patriarchal canon. What opportunities as well as hardships come to the woman who sees herself outside the male company of poets? How can she at once assume their power and make it her own? The opening chapter suggests that a woman poet's awareness of her particular relation to this patriarchal tradition alters her sense of the burdens of the past. By conceiving of herself as necessarily apart from this male line of poets, Dickinson creates a space, a crucial discontinuity, that provides her the freedom to experiment. The most radical verbal experimentation may come, after all, from those poets who feel themselves cast out, who perceive a difference between themselves and the tradition, a difference that separates them in vital ways from their forebears.[6]

The critic who wishes to engage in the analytic enterprise of reevaluating Dickinson's relation to this tradition faces ob-

---

[6] Sandra M. Gilbert, in "Patriarchal Poetry and Women Readers: Reflections on Milton's Bogey" (*PMLA*, Volume 93, Number 3, May 1978, pp. 368-382) raises the related issue of women readers' responses to the Miltonic tradition Whereas Gilbert chooses to emphasize the darker implications of Milton's inhibiting powers, I tend to see the Miltonic presence as enforcing a necessary discontinuity between women poets and the patriarchal tradition, a separation which may prove to be the female version of a poetic "fortunate fall"

Introduction

vious difficulties, for Dickinson characteristically employs obscuring strategies, rhetorical disguises that mask as they simultaneously disclose, poetic relationships too ambivalent to be acknowledged openly. How often has the oblique quality of these hermetic poems led us away from a search for origins; how often their self-reflexive form invited us to restrict our analyses of patterns of reference to the isolate text? When moments of explicit allusiveness do appear, readers may seize upon these rhetorical surfaces, pointing to verbal echoes and narrative borrowings which may actually reveal little of the underlying relation between the text and its generative sources.[7] Consequently, a study such as mine, that attempts to place Dickinson in context, must depend upon the identifications of themes, strategies, and uses of language that unite her poems. By informing such a general vision with close textual analyses, the reader can identify more clearly the dominant structures, the prevailing gestures, which shape Dickinson's problematic relation to her Romantic origins.

To support my assertion that among Dickinson's most crucial confrontations are those with the Romantics, and that her work presents a distinct version of an American Romanticism, it is necessary to travel the "hidden roads that go from poem to poem," to chart individual poetic crossings.[8] Consequently, the method I have chosen here is to examine a number of Dickinson's poems against the texts of the major Romantics and, by reading one poem through another, to observe the specific gestures and turnings by which Dickinson defines herself against her predecessors.

Although my approach is informed by Harold Bloom's theories of poetic influence and I am indebted to his mapping of this method, I diverge from the Bloomian model in two

---

[7] John Evangelist Walsh (*The Hidden Life of Emily Dickinson* [New York: Simon and Schuster, 1971]) uses this method most egregiously. When dealing with a poet as oblique and shrewd as Dickinson, one should be wary of taking superficial echoes at face value, for they may be only rhetorical covers, veils which hide deeper and more ambivalent literary relationships.

[8] Harold Bloom, *The Anxiety of Influence: A Theory of Poetry* (New York: Oxford University Press, 1973), p. 96.

Introduction

crucial ways: first, my argument depends on a close, sustained reading of poems, in an attempt to uncover the specific strategies of subversion Dickinson employs as she separates herself from her precursors. Secondly, my investigation takes into account the fact that the poet at the center of this process is a woman. This crucial difference of gender is not simply a biographical reality. Instead, I maintain that gender identity affects the course of poetic influence itself. While eschewing Bloom's terminology of defense mechanisms and tropes, which would, in any event, have to be radically revised if applied to Dickinson, I nonetheless approach her through other poets. Wordsworth, Keats, Shelley, and Emerson most powerfully represent the tradition of a naturalizing Romanticism, the tradition that Dickinson found at once liberating and impossible to share. The obvious omissions here are Byron and Coleridge, and I want to explain their partial exclusion from the following chapters—a decision based not on these poets' lack of influence on Dickinson but rather on the character of that influence. What this book seeks to identify is Dickinson's reaction to a particular strain in the Romantic imagination: its conceptualization of the poet's relation to the natural world and its characterization of the very act of writing lyric poetry. Although Byron is assuredly one of the Romantic company, his impact on Dickinson most sharply affects her creation of a persona, the dramatization of the poetic self as Romantic artist who vies with heaven and earth for freedom. Although Byron's poetry, in large measure, anticipates Dickinson's dramatic defiance of nature and God's laws, his work remains beyond the scope of this discussion because my primary concern here is with those Romantics whose chief mode is the lyric. Whereas Byron turns to the dramatic narrative to depict the energies of his demonic hero, Dickinson converts the lyric itself into a dramatic form. Dickinson's adaptation of the Byronic persona, her involvement in the transmutation of the Romantic hero's identification with the powers of masculinity, has already begun to be articulated in Sandra M. Gilbert and Susan Gubar's book, *The Madwoman in the Attic: The Woman Writer and the Nineteenth-Century Literary Imagi-*

Introduction

nation, which complements and extends my discussion here. As for Coleridge, his relation to Dickinson might best be illustrated through her appropriation and subversion of what M. H. Abrams calls the "greater Romantic lyric," a form of which Coleridge was the master. Consequently, I incorporate into the chapter on Dickinson and Wordsworth a brief discussion of Coleridge's conversation ode "Frost at Midnight," as the parent text of Dickinson's "The Frost Was Never Seen." Here I relate Dickinson's subversion of the Coleridgean structure, her technical strategies, to the epistemological differences between her and the naturalizing Romantics, a relationship that informs this book's main subject.

Dickinson is, of course, not alone in her reevaluation of the relations between self and word, for standing between her and the major English Romantics is Emerson, whose vision of the Me and the Not Me most closely resembles her own. Dickinson follows him not only in ascribing such powers to the self, but in conceiving of the poet as a reader of the universe, as language-maker. At the same time, however, that she rejects an Emersonian nature which educates man, she proceeds to imagine the world as a deceptive text that cannot be read right, and so must remain a deeply equivocal mystery. Whereas Emerson extolls the power of the Eye, Dickinson is more absorbed by what she cannot see. Therefore the correspondence Emerson asserts between nature and the self breaks down as the landscape becomes either, as Roy Harvey Pearce suggests, the scene for allegorical projections or, as Robert Weisbuch has persuasively argued, the originating scene for Dickinson's anti-allegorical poems.[9] What she strives

---

[9] Roy Harvey Pearce remarks: "When she does directly relate the natural world to her own sense of herself, it is by a kind of allegory, in which self and nature are kept quite separate." (*The Continuity of American Poetry* [Princeton: Princeton University Press, 1961]), p. 178. Robert Weisbuch, however, presents a more complex vision of Dickinsonian allegory, or what he calls, "anti-allegory":

"Because their situations are clearly illustrative and appear potentially encyclopedic, anti-allegories are, in a broad sense, allegorical. They force the reader to seek out causal implications. In search of them, the reader looks to see where the language points, to which authoritative orders In fact, he

Introduction

for, however, is not an Emersonian oneness with the world, a healing of the separation between the Me and the Not Me, so much as a direct, unmediated confrontation with death, from which she hopes to win her privileged vision.

Encouraged by Emerson to explore relentlessly within, Dickinson finds there not the unlimited powers of his fluid and multifarious self, but internal division. What serves Emerson as a source of strength, the solace he discovers, fails her needs. When, in his darkest moments, Emerson sees only "I and the Abyss," he can assume the guise of an overseer who absents himself from the despair of this world to gaze at life with ironic benevolence.[10] This fluid concept of self, a boundless potency, hardens in Dickinson to two—self and its internal adversary. Emersonian power assumes a deeply austere guise in her skeptical and uncompromising imagination.

Reading Dickinson through and against the major Romantics, we realize her reliance upon and divergence from them. The degree to which Dickinson risks all, her quality of radical experimentation, is, I would argue, intimately connected to her sense of herself as estranged from the tradition. Any theory of poetic influences must account for the sex of the poet, and the question of Dickinson's sense of estrangement from the tradition is fundamentally involved with her awareness of her own isolation, and the freedom and particular burdens such an exclusionary relation to the tradition permits. How and to what extent a woman poet defines herself against the patriarchal tradition—if generalizations about women poets can be made at all—are questions of some importance not only for Dickinson and women poets, but for clarifying our

---

may find in the poem many gestures toward such orders, but finally he is forced back by this very plethora of suggestion from a monistic, referential interpretation, forced back to a holistic description of the poem's pattern in terms of nothing but itself." (Robert Weisbuch, *Emily Dickinson's Poetry* [Chicago: The University of Chicago Press, 1972]), p. 48.

[10] See R. A. Yoder, "Toward the 'Titmouse Dimension': The Development of Emerson's Poetic Style," *PMLA*, Volume 87, March 1972, pp. 255-270.

Introduction

notions of canon formation and theoretical interpretations of the dominant tradition.[11] The most direct approach to Dickinson may be the most apparently perverse, for only by reading her in the context of the tradition do we discover, as if for the first time, the poet whose dark courage leads to such radical experimentation. Returning to Dickinson's poems with the voices of Romanticism echoing in our ears, we hear a voice uncompromising in its austerity, at once more familiar than we had formerly chosen to acknowledge, and more strange.

[11] In *Women Writers and Poetic Identity* (Princeton: Princeton University Press, 1980), which appeared after the completion of my manuscript, Margaret Homans perceptively analyzes the principles governing Dickinson's language in terms of her gender. Homans' extremely suggestive insights into the poet's attempts to move beyond sexual distinctions by creating a gender-free discourse and her investigations into the origins of Dickinson's irony will be central to all future discussions of Dickinson as woman poet and of her relationship to the male poetic tradition.

I

"Come Slowly—Eden":
The Woman Poet and Her Muse

> Swedenborg has written that we are each in the midst of a group of associated spirits who sleep when we sleep and become the *dramatis personae* of our dreams, and are always the other will that wrestles with our thought, shaping it to our despite.[1]
>
> —William Butler Yeats

IN HIS RECENT JOURNEYS along the "hidden roads that go from poem to poem," Harold Bloom explores the dilemma of a poet wrestling with his precursors.[2] Bloom has turned to the rhetorical systems of Vico, Nietzsche, Freud, and the Kabbalah to illuminate his own vision. His use of these systems assumes the poet to be male, for the tropes these models offer convey a specific sexual identity. The oedipal struggle, the son's war with the father, the desire for and resentment of the seductive female, must echo throughout these philosophies of origins.[3] Although Bloom keeps alluding to the sexual

---

[1] William Butler Yeats, "Swedenborg, Mediums and the Desolate Places (1914)," in *Explorations* (New York: Macmillan Co., 1962), 1.56.

[2] Harold Bloom, *The Anxiety of Influence: A Theory of Poetry* (New York: Oxford University Press, 1973), p. 96.

[3] Because Freud's paradigm for the male has been so thoroughly explored elsewhere, I mention it here only in terms of Bloom's revision of Freudian theory. Of course Bloom defends himself against charges that his criticism is a reductive Freudian gesture. He has recently argued that "imagination, as Vico understood and Freud did not, is the faculty of self-preservation, and so the proper use of Freud, for the literary critic, is not so to apply Freud (or even revise Freud) as to arrive at an Oedipal interpretation of poetic history. I find such to be the usual misunderstanding that my own work provokes. In studying poetry we are not studying the mind, nor the

13

aspects of the poet's dilemma, he repeatedly avoids the question raised by his own speculations, "What if the poet be a woman?" But how might the process of influence differ for women poets, and how do women poets perceive their relation to a male-dominated tradition?[4] It is to this question that the following chapters will, in various ways, return. For the theoretical framework I set forth here finds its specific examples and strongest justification in the individual chapters, the close readings of Dickinson and the Romantics, that follow. Moreover, what I suggest about the confrontation between Dickinson and the Romantic imagination may be taken to apply more generally to post-Romantic women poets' perceptions of influence in the nineteenth century. Indeed, such

---

Unconscious, even if there is an unconscious. We are studying a kind of labor that has its own latent principles, principles that can be uncovered and then taught systematically" ("Poetry, Revisionism, Repression," *Critical Inquiry* 2, no. 2 [Winter 1975]: 250) My aim is to avoid such a reductive misreading of Bloom's thought and, instead, to examine briefly the assumptions behind the rhetorical forms of his theory in order to arrive at a revised theory of poetic influence for women poets. Such an attempt must be careful to distinguish between the descriptive and prescriptive aspects of any theory that seeks to come to terms with a preexisting tradition. But once the argument is lifted out of a particular context and stands as a paradigm for "how poets make poems," it becomes open to analysis as a poetic construct in its own right; its rhetorical implications deserve close scrutiny. What the theory evades will come back to haunt it.

[4] In *A Map of Misreading* (New York: Oxford University Press, 1975), Bloom writes, "Nor are there Muses, nymphs who *know*, still available to tell us the secrets of continuity, for the nymphs certainly are now departing. I prophesy though that the first true break with literary continuity will be brought about in generations to come, if the burgeoning religion of Liberated Woman spreads from its clusters of enthusiasts to dominate the West. Homer will cease to be the inevitable precursor, and the rhetoric and forms of our literature then may break at last from tradition" (p. 33). The ambivalence behind Bloom's assertion is clear. In the face of a loss of the muses, the male poet is denied his inspiration, the primitive fear of desiccation Ferenczi postulates will be fulfilled, the end of the poetic tradition Bloom has so celebrated will dry up. Such loss breeds a renewed fear and anxiety that manifests themselves in rhetorical defensiveness. Yet in between his defenses Bloom admits that women may now be inheriting power and making it their own. Only women can create the necessary discontinuities to break effectively from the past.

"Come Slowly—Eden"

an investigation into the relationship between women poets and the Romantics demonstrates not only a shared awareness of the burdens of tradition but illustrates as well the development of an alternative line to the dominant male canon, the beginning of a countertradition of post-Romantic women poets.[5] Because Dickinson is central to this revision, she will be my primary subject here, yet the reader should remember that the implications of the following chapters are important for others, especially Elizabeth Barrett Browning and Christina Rossetti.[6] Furthermore, I maintain that Dickinson's perception of influence leads us to a provisional formulation of a paradigm that applies more generally to nineteenth-century women poets as they seek independence from powerful male precursors. For Rossetti and Browning as well as for Dickinson, the precursor becomes a composite male figure; finding themselves heirs to a long succession of fathers, these women share the vision of a father/lover that surpasses individuals. And so for them the composite father is the main adversary.[7]

[5] For a discussion of nineteenth-century women poets' interrelationships, see Ellen Moers's *Literary Women* (New York: Doubleday & Co., 1976).

[6] Dickinson first discovered E. B. Browning when she was a young girl. Of the experience she writes, "I think I was enchanted / When first a sombre Girl— / I read that Foreign Lady— / The Dark—felt beautiful— / And whether it was noon at night— / Or only Heaven—at Noon— / For very Lunacy of Light / I had not power to tell—" (*The Poems of Emily Dickinson*, ed. Thomas H. Johnson [Cambridge, Mass.: Harvard University Press, Belknap Press, 1968], no. 593; all subsequent references to Dickinson's poems are to this edition and will be cited in the text by number). Although Browning did not know Dickinson's work, Christina Rossetti did. Sent a copy of Dickinson's poems, Rossetti remarked, "She *had* (for she is dead) a wonderfully Blakean gift, but therewithal a startling recklessness of poetic ways and means" (*Family Letters of Christina Georgina Rossetti*, pp. 176-77, quoted in Eleanor Walter Thomas, *Christina Georgina Rossetti* [New York: Columbia University Press, 1931]). Thomas also draws a number of comparisons between Rossetti and Dickinson.

[7] However, the serious possibility remains that another, less overt, pattern can be discovered in Dickinson's image of the origins of her creativity, one in which the other is identified as a woman. The female serves Dickinson most often not as direct inspiration but as audience and comforter. Susan Gilbert Dickinson, her sister-in-law, shared more of Dickinson's poems than anyone else during the poet's lifetime. And Dickinson listened to Sue's opin-

"Come Slowly—Eden"

Any discussion of influence should be informed by a more general sense of how the poet confronts basic existential events: life, death, the sources of his or her art. As a poet, Dickinson knew no innocence. Her poems attest to frustrated experience—crucial moments lost or anticipated possibilities rejected. Earlier events narrow her sphere of future action. Examining her past and her childhood, Dickinson recalls no privileged sanctuary. Taught to perceive children as lost souls who must find grace before they can be freed from guilt, she feels exiled, banished by a Calvinist consciousness from the "prenatal" possibility of grace. Unlike the Romantics, she does not recall the "visionary gleam" lost in the process of growth, for it has never been hers. When Dickinson invokes an Edenic garden, anxiety and shame mark her perception. In a letter written toward the end of her life, she states, "In all the circumference of Expression, those guileless words of Adam and Eve never were surpassed, 'I was afraid and hid Myself.' "[8] Critics have compared Dickinson's poems with Blake's *Songs of Innocence and of Experience*, but the comparison must concede an overriding difference—Dickinson writes only songs of experience. Those poems which adopt a vision of the young innocent are often her most searing comments. Noting her dark ironies, Clark Griffith remarks that those poems which assume the guise of innocence actually adopt it as a mask; through such irony and paradox, childlike trust is subverted.[9]

---

ions, although she did not always follow her suggestions. Active women authors provided her with encouraging examples; she was especially interested in their work and seems to have identified them as members of a kind of literary sisterhood in whose triumphs she shared and from whom she gained strength. But the dominating "lover," the desired yet threatening master who retains the power to destroy or give life to the poet is, throughout Dickinson's poems and letters, male.

[8] No. 946, to Mr. and Mrs. E. J. Loomis, Autumn 1884, in *The Letters of Emily Dickinson*, ed. Thomas H. Johnson and Theodora Ward (Cambridge, Mass.: Harvard University Press, Belknap Press, 1958), 3:846. All subsequent references to Dickinson's letters will be to this edition.

[9] Clark Griffith, *The Long Shadow: Emily Dickinson's Tragic Poetry* (Princeton, N. J.: Princeton University Press, 1964), pp. 17-73, *passim*.

"Come Slowly—Eden"

Resentment and anxiety are the mirror emotions which reflect Dickinson's vision of reality. The fear she experiences when contemplating the advent of any possible happiness arises from an already present knowledge, a foreboding which could appear only in one who had experienced, if subliminally, the anguished sum of life's promise. Her distrust of nature and her isolation from mother and God stem from this self-conscious absence of innocence; it depends upon an educated awareness of the experience's potential for destruction and injury. For example, in an early valentine sent to Elbridge G. Bowdoin, Dickinson's vision of erotic bliss is shadowed by her awareness of the other side of life. Within this highly conventional romantic frame, death and the swift punishment of God's law reside.

> The life doth prove the precept, who obey shall happy be,
> Who will not serve the sovreign, be hanged on fatal tree.

The reality principle overwhelms this paean to romance, and the prevailing consciousness creating the poem cannot free itself from death's imminence:

> The *worm* doth woo the *mortal*, death claims a living bride,
> Night unto day is married, morn unto eventide; . . . [1]

A Darwinian relentlessness invades even this instance of coquettish flirtation. Rather than attempt to subsume her anxiety by a posture of feigned innocence, Dickinson may attest to her own wariness. She confronts the apprehension which forces her to pause before accepting experiences of possible pleasure as well as pain.

> Come slowly—Eden!
> Lips unused to Thee—
> Bashful—sip thy Jessamines—
> As the fainting Bee—

"Come Slowly—Eden"

Reaching late his flower,
Round her chamber hums—
Counts his nectars—
Enters—and is lost in Balms. [211]

According to Dickinson, the power of someone outside the self first awakens her from passivity. She depends upon an "other" to answer her call and heed her song. Without a responsive voice, supportive and alluring, she fears that she might lose the impetus to continue to write. Yet this awakening is associated with both the world of books and death. This coupling is hardly coincidental, for words themselves at once "enchant" and "infect" her. They carry a lethal potency akin to the attraction of death, which offers a solution to life's mysteries and the erotic satisfaction of sacrifice, giving one's self to an inscrutable lover. But death renders the soul silent, and communication between the dead and the living proves impossible. The temptation of death arises from Dickinson's need to obviate the frustrations of experience, the fear of death from the defeating silence it imposes.

Dickinson's relation to this muse, the inspiriting force she invokes, adds to her perception of the Master Poet, a symbolic figure who subsumes the individual poets that comprise his identity, and the Composite Precursor, who represents the collective force of the major influences upon her writing. Yet her sense of her muse differs fundamentally from that of the male Romantics, Wordsworth, Keats, Shelley. For them the traditional vision of the feminine goddess, the image of the fecund if idealized or distant muse, lingers. The male poets retain the ability to separate their poetic fathers—mythic progenitors—from the muse. The relation between the male poet and his muse is a private courtship upon which the presence of the father impinges but in which the younger poet, depending upon his strength, may win his muse from the father to invoke the aura of inspiration he desires. The ritual of invocation itself serves as a propitiating gesture, a positive strategy to make one's obeisance to the forces of creativity. But not for Dickinson. Her dilemma of influence is at once complicated and radically simplified by her perception that the Composite Precursor and her muse are the same. The muse gains stature and his or her power increases through this identification. When Dickinson envisions her muse as male, she fears his priapic power and wards him off with intense anxiety as she simultaneously seeks to woo him:

> We shun it ere it comes,
> Afraid of Joy,
> Then sue it to delay
> And lest it fly,
> Beguile it more and more—
> May not this be
> Old Suitor Heaven,
> Like our dismay at thee? [1580]

Although Dickinson does not say here that she is explicitly describing her response to the advent of the muse, she has outlined what for her becomes a typical drama, whether the "it" refers to a season, a lover, or poetic inspiration.

For the male poet, the birth of a poem fulfills his maieutic impulse; he becomes both midwife to and mother of his art. But Dickinson acknowledges a potential shift in psychic responsibility when the poet is a woman, from the self to the doubly potent muse. With this shift comes a heightened anxiety, a fear that the passivity a woman poet had banished may return if the "ephebe" must prostrate herself before a masculine muse. This fear partially accounts for Dickinson's distrust of the visitor, her ambivalent responses toward the figure of the stranger in her poems. So great is the pressure the poet faces that she is tempted to relinquish her poetic ambitions and the power of action. Yet out of her struggle with passivity and retreat comes the triumph of a poem which records the terms of the confrontation:

> I would not paint—a picture—
> I'd rather be the One
> It's bright impossibility

"Come Slowly—Eden"

To dwell—delicious—on—
And wonder how the fingers feel
Whose rare—celestial—stir—
Evokes so sweet a Torment—
Such sumptuous—Despair—

I would not talk, like Cornets—
I'd rather be the One
Raised softly to the Ceilings—
And out, and easy on—
Through Villages of Ether—
Myself endued Balloon
By but a lip of Metal—
The pier to my Pontoon—

Nor would I be a Poet—
It's finer—own the Ear—
Enamored—impotent—content—
The License to revere,
A privilege so awful
What would the Dower be,
Had I the Art to stun myself
With Bolts of Melody! [505]

Note that Dickinson speaks of "dower," the wealth one brings to marriage. If she brought what she has been saving to a wedding of the powers within herself, she would be stunned, struck by bolts (which recall the threatened phallic power of lightning); yet these bolts are made of melody, the music of the poem. Here language reflects the pull of attraction and terror that informs Dickinson's view of independence as a poet and the dangers attendant on creative self-sufficiency.

Dickinson's plea for independence signals another breakdown in the conventional romantic relationship of poet and muse. Implicit in the Romantic view of the poet as quester is a self that pursues the dangerous, seductive female. Masculinity, associated with the active self, the literary voice of authority from the Bible onward, continues its dominance. Most immediately Milton's abiding presence confirms and deepens the masculine tenor of post-Enlightenment poetry. If the Romantics assumed the poet to be a mental "hero," transferring the metaphor of the quest to the vocation of the poet, then the role of the woman was to wait, to taunt the poet with visions of bliss, and, if he were lucky, possibly to lead him beyond the confines of the human into a realm of spiritual awakening accompanied by the punishment of death. Yet for the post-Romantic woman poet the roles of muse and poet have shifted. Because of this transference, Dickinson wavers between feeling that she must wait to receive her Master/muse and radical rejection of his presence. Threat of dependence foments rebellion; by casting off her Precursor, she fears that she may be relinquishing her muse as well. In the process of exorcising her Precursor, she may banish the source of her art. In her late poems, Dickinson asserts her independence of any master, yet she remains haunted by the possibility that she may have been robbed of his potency and power. Her poems vacillate between these two poles—the conflict remains unresolved and so must be reenacted in poem after poem.

> Growth of Man—like Growth of Nature—
> Gravitates within—
> Atmosphere, and Sun endorse it—
> But it stir—alone—
>
> Each—it's difficult Ideal
> Must achieve—Itself—
> Through the solitary prowess
> Of a Silent Life—
>
> Effort—is the sole condition—
> Patience of Itself—
> Patience of opposing forces—
> And intact Belief—
>
> Looking on—is the Department
> Of it's Audience—
> But Transaction—is assisted
> By no Countenance— [750]

"Come Slowly—Eden"

Responsibility for the self can gain ascendancy, but it is an experience that may be temporary—lasting for only a single morning and then undergoing brutal attack:

> My Soul—accused me—And I quailed—
> As Tongues of Diamond had reviled
> All else accused me—and I smiled—
> My Soul—that Morning—was My friend—
>
> Her favor—is the best Disdain
> Toward Artifice of Time—or Men—
> But Her Disdain—'twere lighter bear
> A finger of Enamelled Fire— [753]

Self-reliance can turn into nightmare when the light of internal approval vanishes. When the enemy resides within, the attack is overwhelming, because any mediating distance is absent.[10]

Clearly these poems do not refer specifically to writing poems, but the attitudes they express extend throughout the full range of Dickinson's experiences. The vocation of the poet is one of her prime concerns, not only because she spent her life writing, but because she places the power of the poet above that of the physical world and the act of writing on a plane with God. She establishes her priorities: "I reckon—when I count at all—/First—Poets—Then the Sun—" (569). Indeed the poet must challenge God and wrest a blessing

---

[10] Here Freud's comment on the nature of repression is particularly helpful: "Repression is an attempt at flight on the part of the ego from the libido which it feels to be dangerous; the phobia may be compared to a fortification against the outer danger which now stands for the dreaded libido The weakness of this defensive system in the phobias is of course that the fortress which is so well guarded from without remains exposed to danger from within; projection externally of danger from libido can never be a very sucessful [sic] measure" (Sigmund Freud, *A General Introduction to Psychoanalysis* [New York: Simon & Schuster, 1975], p. 417). If we substitute the libido of Freudian psychology for that part of the self Dickinson associates with the Stranger (which interestingly and correctly underlines the sexual aspects of his identity), the analogous process can be observed in Dickinson's relation to her various selves

from Him. In "A Little East of Jordan," Dickinson describes this process:

> A little East of Jordan,
> Evangelists record,
> A Gymnast and an Angel
> Did wrestle long and hard—
>
> Till morning touching mountain—
> And Jacob, waxing strong,
> The Angel begged permission
> To Breakfast—to return—
>
> Not so, said cunning Jacob!
> 'I will not let thee go
> Except thou bless me'—Stranger!
> The which acceded to—
>
> Light swung the silver fleeces
> 'Peniel' Hills beyond,
> And the bewildered Gymnast
> Found he had worsted God! [59]

Late in life, Dickinson explicitly identified Jacob with the poet, with herself: "Audacity of Bliss, said Jacob to the Angel 'I will not let thee go except I bless thee'—Pugilist and Poet, Jacob was correct—."[11] However, here Dickinson alters the words of Genesis as the poet Jacob assumes the authority over the angel, messenger of God. As Jacob wrestles with the stranger, so Dickinson wrestles with her muse. She associates wrestling not only with receiving God's power and the favors of the muse but also with the process of birth. When congratulating her friend Mrs. Holland upon the birth of a son, she writes, "I pray for the tenants of that holy chamber, the wrestler, and the wrestled for."[12] Dickinson shares in the tradition of poets' identifying their creative role with a woman's giving birth to a child, and she places her

---

[11] Dickinson, letter no. 1042, III, 903, Spring 1886, to T. W. Higginson.

[12] Dickinson, letter no. 210, II, 356, December 1859, to Mrs. J. G. Holland.

emphasis on the physical realities of the process. Despite the fact that as a woman giving birth would be a biological possibility for her, she does not easily fuse the metaphor of birth with artistic creativity, as one might expect. Instead, she stresses her potential vulnerability during poetic "conception" and the physical struggle of the birth process itself.

The physicality of wrestling as a metaphor for poetic creativity relates to Dickinson's sense of struggle when confronting the combined power of muse and male Precursor. This double identity of stranger and preceptor is a source of the continuing ambivalence toward her own powers and the simultaneous need to banish all authorities outside the self. Yet she is frequently abashed by the power of the Precursor, the lover, God. This combined male figure fills her with what she calls "awe," an awareness and fear of the sublimity of her confrontations with the other. In order to accommodate her ambivalence, Dickinson seizes upon moments of gain and loss, of annunciation and departure. Each poem serves as a buffer, a momentary stopping of experience which embodies the control she longs to assert over existence. Writing to her cousins Louise and Frances Norcross, Dickinson explains how she reacts to the deaths which crowded her last years: "Each that we lose takes part of us; / A crescent still abides, . . . I work to drive the awe away, yet awe impels the work."[13]

"Awe," the result and reaction to her private loss, becomes a precondition for her fragmentary form of art. Throughout the poems, Dickinson has continually claimed that anguish and pain of stunning magnitude evoke a commensurate stoicism within her. Through this process of rising to meet life's grim occasions, she creates poems. Though pain may be a necessary precondition for the poet to speak with forthright intensity, such suffering may obliterate the possibility of any communication at all. Overwhelming experience can throw the poet into the stoicism of silence, the relinquishment of her art:

[13] Dickinson, letter no. 891, III, 817, late March 1884, to Louise and Frances Norcross.

"Come Slowly—Eden"

> Give little Anguish—
> Lives will fret—
> Give Avalanches—
> And they'll slant—
> Straighten—look cautious for their Breath—
> But make no syllable—like Death—
> Who only shows his Marble Disc—
> Sublimer sort—than Speech— [310]

At times Dickinson succumbs to the silence she describes, for the precondition of suffering causes her intermittently to shift from silence to her brief poems and back again. One source of this suffering is the tension the poet describes between her need to give herself and fear that her power may be permanently usurped. She forestalls as she welcomes moments of ecstasy—occasions when she is beside herself. Yet she also fears complete self-possession:

> I am afraid to own a Body—
> I am afraid to own a Soul—
> Profound—precarious Property—
> Possession, not optional—
>
> Double Estate—entailed at pleasure
> Upon an unsuspecting Heir—
> Duke in a moment of Deathlessness
> And God, for a Frontier. [1090]

Here the legacy of body and soul has become an agonizing condition; she feels unprepared and defenseless, not ready to face her God—the frontier of immortality that lies on the other side of the "property" she has inherited. Interestingly, the inheritor is a "Duke," the heir a man. The body and soul Dickinson is afraid to own would be the masculine side of a self whose identity she assumes frequently in both her poems and letters.[14]

---

[14] Dickinson repeatedly attempts to internalize the masculine power, for she realizes the vulnerability of her position as someone who must await the

"Come Slowly—Eden"

Another source of anxiety is her need to face this internalized Master so that she may receive the requisite energy to revolt against the trauma that a confrontation of two internal selves provokes.[15] Responding to the negative aspects of the internalized other, Dickinson considers banishing him. But the task is not easy and at times proves impossible:

> Of Consciousness, her awful Mate
> The Soul cannot be rid—
> As easy the secreting her
> Behind the Eyes of God.
>
> The deepest hid is sighted first
> And scant to Him the Crowd—
> What triple Lenses burn upon
> The Escapade from God— [894]

However, when consciousness and self combine, they are able to overcome threatening forces within. A unified identity allows Dickinson to assert her priority over others by placing herself where the preeminent authority had once reigned.[16] As another's power fades, the giver of the word assumes ascendancy. Her power is derived directly from his relinquishment of life. Indeed Dickinson may explicitly reject the voice of another who had earlier fostered a de-

---

male. In order to strengthen herself, she adopts both masculine and feminine identities to escape the dangers of passivity. The degree of internalization of masculine identity varies, one may conjecture, in relation to her level of anxiety. At times, God/father/Master Poet appear so remote as to be unapproachable; in other poems, their power clearly resides within. Such internalization poses its own threat, for Dickinson fears a split self over which she may possess only limited control, an intimacy that may prove lethal. For examples of such masculine identification, see poems 196, 389, 466, 704, and 986. In another letter to Louise and Frances Norcross (no 367, early October 1871 [2:490]), Dickinson signs herself "brother Emily"; and in a letter to Edward Dickinson, she refers to advice her mother gave her when she was "a Boy" (no. 571, about 1878 [2:622]).

[15] See Dickinson's poem "One need not be a Chamber—to be Haunted—" (670).

[16] See Poem 616.

pendency within her. Once she has achieved a capacity to sustain herself, she dismisses him with a peremptory gesture: "Art thou the thing I wanted? / Begone—my Tooth has grown—".[17]

In the male poet's relation to his muse, the third mythic persona is the father who vies with his son for the female's favors. But in Dickinson's confrontation with her art, the father emerges on the side of the other. Not competing with a jealous parent for her lover's attention, she lacks the "stimulus" of rigorous family competition. Instead, the struggle for dominance and loyalty develops between her devotion to Christ/God and this secular lover/muse/poet. Dickinson fears that she may be accused of blaspheming the God who alone should receive her trust. The origins of her sense of herself as blasphemer are in her "unbelief," an estrangement from God's company, and her accusation that her God is a *deus absconditus* whom she seeks but cannot find. Present too in her poems is the guilt of one who substitutes human love for divine. Her skepticism of orthodoxy provides one source of shame. She asks Christ why she suffers and then is embarrassed by her own question. Love for another, the assertion of independence, the exercise of judgment—experiences central to the growth of the soul—intensify her guilt before God. Like so many others, this dilemma is unresolved; instead, the burden of blasphemy enters Dickinson's poems, contributing to her store of guilt. This alarming variation on the process of poetic influence contributes to her fear of being invaded, of allowing herself to be violated while at the same time continuing to court her lover/muse/poet. The triple potency of his power reveals why she could conceive of the word as disease, an infection which had the power to destroy.

A BRIEF EXAMINATION of poems by Christina Rossetti and Elizabeth Barrett Browning presents striking parallels to Dickinson's process of poetic influence. Although each of

---

[17] Poem 1282.

these Victorian female poets differs in the extent of awareness she brings to her dilemma, the strategies they employ serve an analogous purpose. Rossetti exhibits the least self-consciousness about her role as poet; she wrote quickly and rarely revealed any brooding upon her "habit," as she called it, of writing poems. However, her stance of orthodox religiosity, of humble abstemiousness, reveals in its severity her need for increased repression—the necessity of surrounding her art with strictures. On rare occasions such as "Goblin Market," temptation breaks through, and with it the subconscious reveling in unfulfilled desires takes hold of the poem and releases the psychic pressures which otherwise subsume Rossetti's poetic voice. The lush quality of the poem's diction collides with the ostensible repugnance of the fearsome goblins. The dangerous fruits which the goblin men offer two maiden sisters are so delicious that they cannot be resisted. Characteristically, the direction and rhythm Rossetti uses to describe the forbidden is charged with an energy that suggests she is well aware of its appeal.

For Rossetti, the problem of creativity relates to her need to keep libidinous pressures under strict control. The poems move between an advocacy of the stoicism of silence—an image of a virgin tower impervious to all assaults—and a sensuous diction that embraces as it obstensibly rejects erotic temptation. Like Dickinson, Rossetti must maintain a tension between leaving herself open to sources of passion that she identifies with the rapine power of male sexuality and the need to reject all voices that convey such power, even if this means stifling her own. In order to create a viable space within this conflict, she adopts a rhetoric of disguise which allows her to address the forbidden as evil while simultaneously using a language that betrays her awareness of its appeal.[18]

---

[18] For additional examples, see "The Dead City" (*Poetical Works* [Hildensheim: Georg Olms Verlag, 1970], p. 101) and "My Dream" (*ibid.*, p. 315). For an explanation of her rhetorical strategy expressed in riddle form, see "Winter: My Secret" (*ibid.*, 336).

"Come Slowly—Eden"

Elizabeth Barrett Browning, however, more explicitly acknowledges the problem of being a female poet, writing copiously of the development of the feminine artist in the poem that so deeply impressed Dickinson, *Aurora Leigh*. The acute self-consciousness and length of this poem make it less suitable for discussion than "A Musical Instrument," to which Browning ostensibly ascribed no particular moral or symbolic significance. In *Pan the Goat-God: His Myth in Modern Times*, Patricia Merivale comments on Browning's version of Pan. Browning, she writes, "captures better than anyone since Milton '*semicaperque deus: semideusque caper*' [the god half-goat; the goat half-god]—the paradox of Pan's nature; her interpretation of it is that as a beast he is cruel, as a god he is creative. 'Yet half a beast is the great god Pan.' "[19] The poem goes beyond the war between Pan and Christ, the false god and the true. It reveals Browning's resentment of Pan, the goat-god—an image of animalistic masculinity and poetic creator. He is a brute but also the artist forming the instrument for his song—the naturalistic muse of pagan ancestry who had repeatedly to subjugate his song to the spiritual power of Jesus. The strength of this short poem, in contrast to the often sentimental, overly self-deprecating *Sonnets from the Portuguese* or the forced poems of social concern, demonstrates an antithetical strain in Browning's poetry. Resentment leaves its mark upon her despite her overt stance of dependence and sacrifice. In this poem, Pan appears less an advocate of the natural than its destroyer. He spreads "ruin" and scatters "ban," breaking the lilies and disrupting the peace of the river; he is the goat-god come to ravage a vision of pastoral sanctity. With astounding arrogance, Pan sits "high on the shore" and fashions his instrument, whittling away at the patient reed with "his hard bleak steel." He cuts it short and removes its pith, all for the sake of playing his tune. His conscience untouched, Pan admires his work, for this is

[19] Patricia Merivale, *Pan the Goat-God: His Myth in Modern Times* (Cambridge: Harvard University Press, 1969), pp. 83-84.

"*Come Slowly—Eden*"

> 'The only way, since gods began
> To make sweet music, they could succeed.'

Past analyses of the poem have neglected the fact that these lines appear in quotation marks; they represent Pan's song and not the poet's sentiments. These readings fail to differentiate between his voice and the voice of the poet, who does not necessarily concur in the idea that through destruction alone can artists create. The true gods sigh at the sight, the price of Pan's creativity; they do not gleefully acquiesce in his destruction of the pastoral vision. His final achievement, the song, is indeed sweet; nature itself is brought back to life through Pan's music. But the poem does not end in tranquil reconciliation:

> Yet half a beast is the great god Pan,
>   To laugh as he sits by the river,
> Making a poet out of a man:
> The true gods sigh for the cost and pain,—
> For the reed which grows nevermore again
>   As a reed with the reeds in the river.

The poet is the pithed reed, diminished to serve better as the instrument of the muse—the creative, inspiriting breath which blows through him. Browning reminds us that the sacrifice of the reed, the man, must be remembered in the song and that the true gods, the true poets, are constant to the effort art has cost them. What is unique in this characterization of Pan is his brutish, bestial, highly individualized identity. The Wordsworthian Pan was a more general spirit, an arcadian ideal.[20] As Merivale demonstrates, Browning veers away from the Romantic image of the rather dematerialized Pan and restores to him his bestial origins. Her resentment of the brute, masculine, destructive force Pan embodies suggests a hidden resentment of the male poet, the creator to whom she so frequently paid obeisance in her

---

[20] See *The Prelude*, bk. 8, lines 180 ff.

"Come Slowly—Eden"

other poems. *A Musical Instrument* demonstrates the fusion in her mind of the destructive, the bestial, and the masculine with the muse/poet, an image she describes with antagonistic bitterness.

I do not contend that Dickinson, Rossetti, and Browning reveal identical pressures. However, each poem cited does embody similar tensions: a sense of struggle, an awareness of the expense—of what is lost—in the process of attaining one's own poetic voice.[21] Each poet sacrifices a part of herself, relinquishes an aspect of her psyche, to be able to write. What distinguishes this drama from the masculine poet's perception of influence is that for these women the antithetical force is a male tempter: stranger, goblin, or Pan. He is dreaded despite his attractiveness, feared when he is confronted. Yet the differences among these emblematic texts are as instructive as the similarities. Although these poets perceive the masculine persona in terms of temptation and denial, each asserts the drama in a different guise and plays a different role in it. For Rossetti, renunciation means a rejection of sexual temptation for the strictly religious life; in obedience she finds a fulfillment of her subjugated longing. There is little subjective evaluation of her role as artist; she envisions her tempter not as poet but as goblin—part animal, part man. In the watercolor drawings which illustrate the poem, Rossetti paints the goblin's feet and hands in bestial forms, a visual image akin to Browning's verbal portrait of Pan.[22] But Browning's identity as an artist is more clearly defined. She at once proclaims her devotion to the superior

---

[21] For helpful, if too brief, remarks on repression and the nineteenth-century woman poet, see Adrienne Rich, "Vesuvius at Home: The Power of Emily Dickinson," *Parnassus: Poetry in Review* 5, no. 1 [Fall-Winter, 1976], p. 66.

[22] The goblins, part beast and part myth, share the spirit and identity of Pan. Discussing the classical conception of Pan, Joseph Campbell (*The Hero with a Thousand Faces* [Cleveland: World Publishing Co., 1949], p. 81) writes that the goat-god was perceived as a "dangerous presence dwelling just beyond the protected zone of the village boundary." So too, Christina Rossetti's goblins live beyond the town, in the dangerous natural world of temptation.

lover/poet while at the same time she attests to her role as a striving poet who seeks independence. Her most ambitious poem describes the pain and effort of just such a heroine-poet who enacts the process of self-discovery. Dickinson's "romance," as I have suggested earlier, cannot be separated from her relation to the lover/muse/poet. In her work, the fusion of woman and poet is strong, the identity established. Both inhabit the same emotional realm, and it is this fusion which forms the "chief intensity" of her poetry.

Any theory of influence must, as it should now be clear, account for the sex of the poet. By touching on the work of Rossetti and Browning in relation to Dickinson's perception of influence, I suggest that the constellation of the "family romance" alters when the poet is a woman—that recognition of the particular pressures upon women poets when they face their necessarily composite precursors leads to a more informed reading of these poets. And for Dickinson at least, there is little doubt not only that such a constellation of forces exists but that the process repeatedly arrests her attention. Her poems provide overwhelming proof of the taut balance she strives to maintain between independence and the power of the Precursor/father. She responds to his call and envisions him as the origin and source of her poems. She is constantly tested under the pressure of an all-seeing, invisible scrutiny:

> Tried always and Condemned by thee
> Permit me this reprieve
> That dying I may earn the look
> For which I cease to live— [1559]

Dickinson refuses either renunciation or subjection. She relinquishes her identity to no intruder, and the resulting struggle remains unresolved. The paralyzing ambivalence she feels facing person, Precursor, or death results from the psychic resonance of confrontation. When she writes her final letter to the Norcross cousins, she alludes to a book she received a few months earlier. Borrowing another's words

"Come Slowly—Eden"

for the last time, Dickinson once again lends them an immediacy the author did not intend; of her approaching death she writes, "Called Back!" As she faces death, Dickinson finds herself answering another's call, listening to the mysterious voice, facing yet another presence. Against his summons, she asserts her final power—she utters death's own command. This subversion culminates a lifetime of confrontations with the *personae* who sleep when she sleeps, who haunt her dreams. She speaks not only of her response but also for that other will that wrestles with her thoughts and from whom she struggles to win brief moments of art:

> He was my host—he was my guest,
> I never to this day
> If I invited him could tell,
> Or he invited me.
>
> So infinite our intercourse
> So intimate, indeed,
> Analysis as capsule seemed
> To keeper of the seed. [1721]

II

Wordsworthian Nature and the Life Within

> Say what some poets will, Nature is not so much her own eversweet interpreter, as the mere supplier of that cunning alphabet, whereby selecting and combining as he pleases, each man reads his own peculiar lesson according to his own peculiar mind and mood. —Herman Melville, *Pierre*

> Wrestling I will not let Thee go,
> Till I thy Name, thy Nature know
> —Charles Wesley (hymn)

DICKINSON'S primary confrontation is, to borrow Emerson's language, between the Me and the Not Me. Consequently, although she shares with the naturalizing Romantics, preeminently Wordsworth, an abiding concern with the relationship between self and world, the power of her poems comes, not from any perceived reciprocity, but rather from the struggle she describes between two competing forces: the individual consciousness and all that is external to it. Awareness of how Dickinson distinguishes her relationship to nature from Wordsworth's reciprocal vision deepens our understanding of her poems' origins as well as their subversive strength.

Crucial to Wordsworth's faith in nature is what Geoffrey Hartman describes as "that double generosity of Nature toward man and man toward Nature, always present in the impassioned Wordsworth."[1] The poet, open and receptive,

---

[1] Geoffrey Hartman, *The Unmediated Vision. An Interpretation of Wordsworth, Hopkins, Rilke, and Valery* (New York: Harcourt, Brace, & World, Inc., 1966), p. 10.

listens to a communicative, often an arrestingly eloquent, landscape; the mind is "willing to work and to be wrought upon."[2] Dickinson, instead, will either appropriate the landscape by internalizing it, or, obversely, deny the boundaries between self and nature by describing the landscape in the anatomical language of arteries and veins, impressing herself upon the land. Either strategy expresses aggression, the need to win dominance from a competing, potentially destructive, province located in the land. In contrast, the Wordsworthian poet's relation to nature is distinguished by his own passivity; he envisions his role as that of a responsive yet calm observer who accepts but does not actively pursue the gift of special insight he receives from the land—moments of communication are marked by an aura of rest and receptivity. "Wordsworth's understanding," to cite Hartman again, "is characterized by the general absence of the will to relational knowledge, that is, knowledge which may be obtained in direct answer to the Why, the What, the Wherefore, and the How."[3]

Thus the poet rescues the crucial, evocative moment from its imminent demise in the natural landscape by transposing the scene from vision to language;[4] nature speaks with awesome boldness forming the "Characters of the great Apocalypse, / The types and symbols of Eternity."[5] If the poet is essential to the relationship of landscape and observer, it is because he recognizes these "types" and "symbols" and, through language, raises the scene from the temporal to a discreet life of its own in the poem. The individual spot of time receives a new permanence from the poet, whose role is both commemorative and salvatory. By fulfilling the promise of the landscape's inherent eloquence, he effects the transition of an ephemeral reciprocity into art. Answering

[2] William Wordsworth, *The Prelude*, Bk. XIV, 1. 103 The edition of Wordsworth's poetry used throughout this chapter is *Wordsworth: Poetical Works*, ed. Thomas Hutchinson, rev. Ernest De Selincourt (London: Oxford University Press, 1969).

[3] Hartman, p. 5.   [4] *Ibid.*, p. 35.

[5] Wordsworth, *The Prelude*, Bk VI, 11. 638-39.

the question "What is a Poet," Wordsworth defines him as a man: "who rejoices more than other men in the spirit of life that is in him; delighting to contemplate similar volitions and passions as manifested in the goings-on of the Universe, and habitually impelled to create them where he does not find them."[6] The note of supreme subjectivity in Wordsworth's last phrase indicates the responsibility which lies with the poet. The generative force when nature is found lacking, he becomes the creative eye that often shapes the scenes he sees. For him "the rocks / Immutable, and everflowing streams, . . . were speaking monuments."[7] Dickinson, however, subverts Wordsworth's "wise passiveness," for she demands of the natural world a coherence and morality which will definitively reveal the character of its creator. Experiencing herself as essentially apart from and in competition with a natural world that holds the promise of decay and death, Dickinson refuses to submit to its arbitrary, time-bound cycles. Not for her the wedding between the poet's ego and nature as bride. Instead, Dickinson's search becomes epistemological as she pushes against the limits of knowledge, asking questions which receive at best gnomic, veiled replies. Rather than the reciprocity between poet and nature which characterizes the ideal state for Wordsworth, Dickinson perceives a damning division between herself and the surrounding landscape. Her moments of epiphany, of naturalistic annunciation, are times of struggle and often acute pain. Aggression dominates as the poet attempts to wrest from nature the power to create her poems. Dickinson fundamentally redirects Wordsworth's relational notion of intermittent epiphanies, for she wants a final, an apocalyptic decision which will yield to her once and for all the gift of visionary power.

The "silent spectacle—the gleam— / The shadow—and the peace supreme!"[8] Wordsworth describes in an "Evening

---

[6] Wordsworth, "Preface," *Lyrical Ballads*, cited by M. H. Abrams, *The Mirror and the Lamp: Romantic Theory and The Critical Tradition* (New York: W. W. Norton & Co , 1958), p. 55.

[7] Wordsworth, *The Prelude*, Bk. VIII, 11. 170-72.

[8] Wordsworth, "Evening Voluntary IX," i. 11. 19-20.

Voluntary," "Composed upon an Evening of extraordinary Splendour and Beauty," is a twilight pervaded by harmony and calm. The tranquillity of nature extends to the poet, who experiences a glimpse of the sublime possibilities of "what can be!"[9] The "exquisite" clarity of the scene unites great distances into a single vision, and this wondrous evening has its origins in other worlds, not natural but divine. The clarity of the scene is not literal but metaphorical; actually the landscape is covered by one of those diaphanous Wordsworthian hazes which adds an aura of peace to the twilight. Viewing the hills bathed in this dreamlike light, the poet envisions Jacob's ladder connecting earth to heaven; the imagination links the visionary landscape to Jacob's own dream. In this "transcendent hour," the poet feels the peace of the scene and invokes a connection between earth and heaven. The intensity of his transcendent vision reminds Wordsworth of his childhood glimpses of glory, renewing his faith in the goodness of the Dread Power of creation. This vision is the poet's "second birth"—the light which once shone through nature reappears and then

> 'Tis past, the visionary splendour fades;
> And night approaches with her shades.[10]

The visionary Jacob's ladder, we are told in a note following the poem, was caused by the haze, and this is literally and figuratively true. As both suggestion and veil, the mists served to spur Wordsworth's imagination. When the light fades, night cloaks the poet in the shadows of the day's mortality. Fleetingly, Wordsworth has witnessed and created an affirmation of the imagination's ability to respond to the natural world with a vision of reaffirmative power. The lost power he mourns in the "Intimations Ode" is briefly captured, and with it the sense of its inevitable fragility returns. This poem combines the two movements Hartman sees as central to Romantic poets: "To explore the transition from self-consciousness to imagination, and to achieve that tran-

[9] *Ibid.*, 1. 8.   [10] *Ibid.*, iv, 1. 79.

sition while exploring it (and so to prove it still possible). . . ."[11] Wordsworth retains his self-awareness, the knowledge that his vision is fleeting and also that this capacity to respond allows him a moment of transcendence. But he knows, too, how much he has lost and how brief this respite will be. Thus, he maintains his acute self-awareness while simultaneously remaining open and receptive to what he sees. His mind works on the landscape and is infused by the harmony and peace of nature; he observes the ridges, transformed by haze, and envisions a ladder, symbol of his inner sensation of connection to and the momentary accessibility of God. Self-consciousness gives way to imagination, and the potency of his vision releases him only to fall anew into the self-conscious pain of lost power and death.

Dickinson, however, is not so willing to relinquish the privileged vision awarded by the annunciatory moment. In "A Little East of Jordan," (poem 59) she draws on Genesis as Wordsworth had done for his image of Jacob's Ladder, and her choice of text reveals her bias.[12]

In the passage to which Dickinson's poem alludes, Jacob confronts and wrestles with the Angel, God's emissary. The battle between the Angel of the Lord and Jacob lasts through the night, and Jacob's triumph signals the dawn. The light of these hills, "silver fleeces," is reminiscent of the Wordsworthian pastoral vision of grazing sheep and rolling landscape, but the tone conveys miracle and surprise. Crucial to the poem and its divergence from Wordsworth is that the bewildered gymnast has *worsted* God. Years after writing the poem, Dickinson was to identify Jacob with the poet, and clearly "A Little East of Jordan" takes as its subject a poet's birth, for it describes the struggle she thought essential be-

---

[11] Geoffrey Hartman, "Romanticism and 'Anti-Self-Consciousness,' " in *Romanticism and Consciousness: Essays in Criticism*, ed. Harold Bloom (New York: W. W. Norton & Co., Inc., 1970), p. 53.

[12] See Emily Dickinson, Poem 59, *The Poems of Emily Dickinson*, ed. Thomas H. Johnson (Cambridge: The Belknap Press of Harvard University Press, 1968), I, 44. The text of this poem appears on p. 23 of the preceding chapter.

fore the individual imagination could *wrest* from God the power to create poems. Both this poem and Wordsworth's "Voluntary" delineate a process which characterizes each poet's predominant vision of the relationship between the self and the "Dread Power." In Dickinson's, however, the focus shifts from the place of struggle to the golden dawn, whereas, in Wordsworth's, the landscape, a sense of place, provides the initial impetus for his renewed vision. "A Little East of Jordan" begins in the night of the soul where Wordsworth's poem ends, and the vision of nature does not precipitate but *follows* a direct confrontation. It is through discord, not harmony, through wrestling, not quiet affirmation, that Dickinson's Jacob witnesses the coming of a new day. Although in both poems the ultimate authority is supranatural, in Dickinson's poem this authority is seized by Jacob; and it is he, stunned, who wins supremacy. Ironically, Wordsworth's poem, emanating strength, harmony, and light, ends with the sinking of his imaginative union into darkness; while Dickinson's struggle with the Angel, a fight that will brook no interruption, closes in the dawn of a newly won poetic power.[13]

[13] Thomas H. Johnson also sees this poem as a direct statement of how the poet conceived of the process of becoming an artist. He remarks:

"The daemonic force that now possessed her she might or might not be able to master, and she saw the challenge quite literally as a wrestling match. Even as early as 1859 she had used it as a theme in her poem 'A Little East of Jordan.' When Jacob waxed strong, the Angel begged for a respite:

> Not so, said cunning Jacob!
> 'I will not let thee go
> Except thou bless me'—Stranger!

The story of how Jacob wrestled with God and was thereby both blessed and disabled she recalled at the conclusion of the scholar-teacher relationship that she maintained with Colonel Higginson for nearly a quarter of a century. In the early spring of 1886, shortly before her death, she wrote Higginson a letter which she intended him to understand would be her farewell message. She comments on her increasing illness and concludes with a note of affectionate remembrance for him and his family: 'Audacity of Bliss, said Jacob to the Angel "I will not let thee go except I bless thee"—Pugilist and Poet, Jacob was correct—' Here the blessing is playfully bestowed by Emily herself, the departing one, an audacious Jacob, who remained to the end a

Wordsworthian Nature

Wordsworth clarifies his vision of the complex relation between the imagination and the natural world in his "Preface" to the 1814 edition of *The Excursion*.[14] Here he asserts that "the Mind of Man" is the "haunt, and the main region of [his] song." Wordsworth, wary of such total solipsism, balances this assertion with a vision of nature blending with mind. As long as his concern is essentially that of a poet seeking to describe the sources of his art, nature plays a central role in the growth and development of the poet's mind; self and world balance to form the poem.

> For the discerning intellect of Man,
> When wedded to this goodly universe
> In love and holy passion, shall find these
> A simple produce of the common day.
> —I, long before the blissful hour arrives,
> Would chant, in lonely peace, the spousal verse
> Of this great consummation:—and, by words
> Which speak of nothing more than what we are,
> Would I arouse the sensual from their sleep
> Of Death, . . .[15]

Mind and world unite; thus the power arising from such a union is regenerative, for "blended might" can will a new

---

fighter for her way of poetry." (*Emily Dickinson: An Interpretative Biography* [Cambridge: The Belknap Press of Harvard Univ. Press, 1955], p. 74).

[14] The Dickinson Collection at the Houghton Library at Harvard University includes a copy of *The Poetical Works of Wordsworth*, ed. Henry Reed (Philadelphia: Hayes & Zell, 1854). In this book, thin pencil lines mark off two passages in the *Excursion*:

> Now to forestall such knowledge as may be
> More faithfully collected from
>   himself   (Bk II, "The Solitary")
>
> Recovered; or if hitherto unknown,
> Lies within reach, and one day shall be
>   given.   (Bk. IV, "Despondency Corrected")

This edition contains *The Prelude*, Bks. I-XIV, as well as *The Excursion*

[15] Wordsworth, "Preface to the Edition of 1814," *The Excursion*, 11. 52-61.

creation. Wordsworth affirms the reciprocity of World and Mind which fit together to accomplish "this our high argument." Moreover, Wordsworth calls upon the Miltonic "prophetic Spirit" to provide the "gift of genuine insight" that enables his own poem to become a source of light and strength.[16] Poets join together in a common pursuit, each with his particular vision. For Dickinson, however, the mode of poetic reciprocity is neither peaceful nor benign. Indeed poetic reciprocity gives way to a struggle between the poet and a formidable adversary who wounds as he bestows his blessing.

In Wordsworth's ideal,

> . . . Poets, even as Prophets, each with each
> Connected in a mighty scheme of truth,
> Have each his own peculiar faculty,
> Heaven's gift, a sense that fits him to perceive
> Objects unseen before, . . .[17]

This "sense" that lends the poet a new vision focuses on the natural world; and this relation between sense and world in Wordsworth is not at all static. Rather, the complexity of his poems derives from a continuing dialogue between self and nature, and the poems reflect the varying degrees of influence which nature and the poet exercise over one another. Although Wordsworth may assert the imagination's ultimate supremacy over the external world, he still finds the source for his inspiration in the landscape. The fundamental distinction between his dialogue and Dickinson's is that Wordsworth vies for power with a nature that promises to yield up its joy and salvation to a sympathetic imagination, whereas Dickinson transforms this striving into an essentially adversarial relationship, with nature often assuming the guise of intrusive, hostile enemy. Nature assumes this role as soon as Dickinson demands that it yield up its secret, that it refer to and illuminate something beyond itself. When Dickinson de-

[16] *Ibid.*, 1. 88
[17] Wordsworth, *The Prelude*, Bk. XIII, 11. 301-304

fines the relationship as epistemological, she questions a nature perceived as an antagonistic force that must be subdued in order to be understood. This is the most extreme form of her skeptical approach to nature, and certainly it is by no means her sole relationship with the natural world; but it is important nonetheless because it illuminates the aggressive and defiant aspects of the imagination's relation to nature which are inherent but covert in Wordsworth's more benign vision.

Even in poems which take as their source a purely "neutral" subject such as a flower or bee, Dickinson charges her language with private anxieties and an awareness of the destructive aspects of nature.[18] Repeatedly, she insists upon her need to control and dominate the natural world. When such domination proves impossible, Dickinson posits an alternative, internal landscape created and controlled by her imagination. Nature not only threatens the poet, it haunts her with a taunting vision of an un-self-conscious existence. The poems of bee and flower form a critique of the alien nature she sees. For, although the poet views the bee with awe and envy, she also knows that, unlike this insect, her life is based on self-awareness, and that the anxiety she feels is an inevitable result of this self-consciousness.

THE GULF between a sentient being and an unthinking nature cannot be bridged by an act of the imagination without altering the forms of nature itself. Dickinson recognizes the need to guard against nature, to watch it warily; she acknowledges its "dread power" more than its pastoral possibilities. Because of this distrust, her writing conveys a sense of being spurred, not by a visible or aural experience, but by a psychological reaction to an intensely human, private event—a death or departure—with nature playing a rhetori-

[18] See Poem 1436, "A Route of Evanescence," for a purely descriptive treatment of the hummingbird's flight. But, often, even such subjects serve to dramatize internal conflict. For a discussion of Dickinson's use of bird, bee, and flower see the chapter that follows.

cal rather than a generative role. Dickinson listens to internal voices as nature falls outside her primary concern:

> The Spirit is the Conscious Ear.
> We actually Hear
> When We inspect—that's audible—
> That is admitted—Here—
>
> For other Services—as Sound—
> There hangs a smaller Ear
> Outside the Castle—that Contain—
> The other—only—Hear— (733)

Spirit, "the conscious ear," participates in an internal dialogue and only secondarily calls upon the voices of nature to translate into sounds understandable to the "smaller ear" and to others "outside the castle," the inchoate dialogue occurring within. When nature does appear in these poems, it functions as analogue not inspiration:

> Growth of Man—like Growth of Nature—
> Gravitates within—
> Atmosphere, and Sun endorse it—
> But it stir—alone—
> . . . . (750)

In his excellent discussion of this poem, Albert Gelpi comments on Dickinson's solipsistic inclinations and their Romantic origins:
"No matter how far or in what direction the process led, the Romantic mind began with the assertion that (in Thoreau's words) 'I only know myself as a human entity; the scene, so to speak, of thoughts and affections . . .' Knowledge was the realization of the self—ideally a complete awareness of one's thoughts and affections. Hence 'the poet is he that hath fat enough, like bears and marmots, to suck his claws all winter. He hibernates in this world, and feeds on his own marrow. . . .' So for Emily Dickinson the romp

in the pasture's living grass was an experience that pertained to a central activity within; in fact, all experience finally mattered only as it modified the self: . . ."[19]

As Gelpi suggests, Dickinson chooses to emphasize the sphere of the Self, rather than to acknowledge the reciprocity between Self and World which informs Wordsworth's more hopeful vision. Such a crucial difference between Wordsworth's reciprocal vision of the natural world with its votive possibilities and Dickinson's essentially adversarial attitude toward nature is most tellingly illustrated in her adaptation of the "inscription" as a poetic theme, simultaneously implicating technique and subject in her skepticism. The process of inscription, the impress of signs on physical objects, undergoes a radical transformation in Dickinson's poems, one which develops from her attempt to free herself of any dependence on an external reality. Compare her use of "endorsement" to the tradition of inscriptions and engravings so popular among English poets in the eighteenth century as it culminates in Wordsworth's "Inscriptions" and "Epitaphs and Elegiac Pieces." Before its transformation by the Romantics, the genre in England was based on the identification of the inscription to the object on which it was inscribed: "The inscription was anything *conscious of the place on which it was written,* and this could be tree, rock, statue, gravestone, sand, window, album, sundial, dog's collar, back of fan, back of painting."[20] Wordsworth moves toward a transformation of this mode. As Hartman suggests: ". . . he made the nature-inscription into a free-standing poem, able to commemorate any feeling for nature or the spot that had aroused this feeling."[21] The Romantic nature-inscription imbues nature with a power to speak directly. Such "iconic and animating gestures as Behold, See, Mark" draw the

---

[19] Gelpi, *Emily Dickinson: The Mind of the Poet* (Cambridge: Harvard University Press, 1966), p. 95.

[20] Geoffrey Hartman, "Wordsworth, Inscriptions, and Romantic Nature Poetry," *From Sensibility to Romanticism,* ed. Frederick W. Hilles and Harold Bloom (New York: Oxford University Press, 1965), p. 390.

[21] *Ibid.,* p. 391.

stranger or traveller to the spot;[22] and "Nature is herself a larger graveyard inscribed deeply with evidences of past life."[23] Dickinson retains these resonances; but the place, the stone on which the inscription is written, becomes not an external, identifiable location existing in the landscape but the soul of the poet. This is a clear instance of Dickinson's startling power to absorb and transform the Romantic tradition of language into a vision of the word which adheres to the identity of the exclusive Self. She becomes the graveyard, the record, the tombstone; nature is no longer the center of remembrance: "The setting is understood to contain the writer in the act of writing: the poet in the grip of what he feels and sees, and primitively inspired to carve it in the living rock."[24] Dickinson's setting is the self—the writer writing. Her own mind and heart become the "living rock" into which experience, pain, and love are engraved:

> I've dropped my Brain—My Soul is numb—
> The Veins that used to run
> Stop palsied—'tis Paralysis
> Done perfecter on stone.

This psychic paralysis, the death of sensate feeling, is wrought into the stone of the self:[25]

[22] Ibid., p. 394.   [23] Ibid., p. 392.
[24] Ibid., p. 400.
[25] In *Emily Dickinson's Poetry: Stairway of Surprise* (New York: Holt, Rinehart and Winston, 1960), p. 211, Charles R. Anderson analyzes "After great pain, a formal feeling comes," and he briefly investigates images of crystallization and the importance of the stone for Dickinson:

"As the images of a funeral rite subside, two related ones emerge to body forth the victim who is at once a living organism and a frozen form. Both are symbols of crystallization: 'Freezing' in the snow, which is neither life nor death but both simultaneously; and 'A Quartz contentment like a stone,' for the paradoxical serenity that follows intense suffering. This recalls her envy of the 'little Stone,' happy because unconscious of the exigencies that afflict mortals, and points forward to the paradox in another poem, 'Contented as despair.' Such is the 'formal feeling' that comes after great pain. It is, ironically no feeling at all, only numb rigidity existing outside time and space."

> Vitality is Carved and cool.
> My nerve in Marble lies—
> A Breathing Woman
> Yesterday—Endowed with Paradise.
>
> Not dumb—I had a sort that moved—
> A Sense that smote and stirred—
> Instincts for Dance—a caper part—
> An Aptitude for Bird—

Dickinson is transformed from a moving, vital being into a piece of marble. Her one hope is the possibility of straining free from this metamorphosis, of a return to what she had been before the unknown witchcraft of this deathlike force fixed her movements and destroyed her life.

> Who wrought Carrara in me
> And chiselled all my tune
> Were it a Witchcraft—were it Death—
> I've still a chance to strain
>
> To Being, somewhere—Motion—Breath—
> Though Centuries beyond,
> And every limit a Decade—
> I'll shiver, satisfied. (1046)

This hope of the spirit echoes the Christian doctrine of the resurrection. Dickinson has adopted the extreme language of the grave to characterize her unnamed crisis. And in the transfer of the action of carving on marble from the stone to the self, Dickinson lends the gesture sexual connotations. Someone, the mysterious "Who" of the poem, has etched his mark on her. Rendered senseless by this act, she can escape only after centuries of struggle. The lurid intimacy of the image conveys an assault upon the self, frightening to contemplate. While Dickinson's sexual anxieties appear in the many poems where she is accosted, wounded, and abandoned to a numbness following pain, they culminate in the image of carving upon the marble of the self.

Wordsworthian Nature

The analogue of self as stone, however, is not reserved exclusively for the effect someone else has wrought. In an early poem, written in 1860, Dickinson imagines herself after death:

> If I should'nt be alive
> When the Robins come,
> Give the one in Red Cravat,
> A Memorial crumb.
>
> If I could'nt thank you,
> Being fast asleep,
> You will know I'm trying
> With my Granite lip! (182)

The granite lip, rendered incapable of speech, is controlled by a "will" which supersedes the body's capacity to respond—effort outlasts mortality. The struggle of the granite lip to speak after death acknowledges the effort of the vital being as it confronts the pressures that urge her into silence; hence the need of another voice, the voice of the reader, who wins the poet's stifled thanks for carrying out the generous task of giving a crumb to a bird, the "memorial crumb" which keeps the poet's memory alive. When she extends this identification of self and stone, Dickinson defines psychic numbing in words charged with eschatological force; as in "After great pain, a formal feeling comes—" (poem 341), where "The Nerves sit ceremonious, like Tombs—" and "The stiff Heart questions was it He, that bore, / And Yesterday, or Centuries before?" Oblivion and loss of feeling mark this internal crisis. Dickinson places the self on an empty stage, externalizing not feelings but their physical locations. She peoples the landscape with her own body to create a graveyard made of the nerves, brain, arteries of the self. Here, too, death is the single trope which can convey this merging of self into stone, a numbing that effects a radical emptying out of the physical organs of self into a space void of direction. The self becomes a graveyard in which

"The Feet, mechanical, go round—," where the diachronic movements of life lose all meaning. A poem ostensibly describing a brilliant Fall reveals a related process of transfusing the language of the body into the external landscape:

> The name—of it—is 'Autumn'—
> The hue—of it—is Blood—
> An Artery—upon the Hill—
> A Vein—along the Road—
>
> Great Globules—in the Alleys—
> And Oh, the Shower of Stain—
> When Winds—upset the Basin—
> And spill the Scarlet Rain—
>
> It sprinkles Bonnets—far below—
> It gathers ruddy Pools—
> Then—eddies like a Rose—away—
> Upon Vermillion Wheels— (656)

Blood, artery, vein, globules, scarlet rain combine to form a surrealistic vision of the human body projected onto the land—an oddly antithetical paean to the brilliance of a New England autumn. Dickinson's alternative strategies of internalization or externalization prove the power of the controlling imagination which does with nature what it will. She abandons the reciprocity Wordsworth sought in favor of the aggrandizement of the mind—a consolidation of power into the self.

Although Wordsworth might have hesitated before these poetic experiments, the germ of Dickinson's method can be found in his own infusion of the powers of a less literal imagination into the landscape. Discussing the "epitaphic origin" and "elegiac tenor" of "Tintern Abbey," Hartman analyzes the process that Dickinson so radically transforms: "the corpse is in the poet himself, his consciousness of inner decay, and the history he meditates is of nature's relation to his mind. We recognize the archaic setting purified of hortative tombstone. The power to make him remember his end or his beginning springs simply and directly from a consciousness involved with nature."²⁶ Dickinson absorbs the Romantic poet's conscious involvement with nature, but she intensifies and literalizes this relationship. Nature becomes alternately a storehouse from which she takes objects to invest them with personal, allegorical significance or she sees it as the place across which she spreads self, blood, vital life.

In "Guilt and Sorrow Or Incidents Upon Salisbury Plain," Wordsworth comes closest to Dickinson's transposition of self into landscape. At the poem's opening, the tortured traveller views a landscape which echoes the guilt he suffers, and the scene reflects the brooding consciousness of this gentle murderer. The "vacant . . . huge waste" which surrounds him provides a barren field for his misery.²⁷ This "dreary place" is transformed, however, when the wanderer meets a fellow sufferer, and the scene shifts from the desolate plain to a cottage, home of communal concern, where the sailor is reunited with his dying wife.²⁸ The stark landscape Wordsworth creates to reflect the wanderer's grief is still susceptible to repentance and sympathy. What distinguishes this treatment of landscape from Dickinson's is Wordsworth's insistence upon retaining the limits of man's power to alter what he sees. Nature in "Salisbury Plain" still participates in the tradition of pathetic fallacy; the man finds his own reflection in the land. But, in Dickinson's poems, the land *becomes* the self as the division between identity and scene dissolves. In one of the most dramatic examples of this identification, Dickinson appropriates the smoldering force of the seemingly silent rock as a symbol for the self; she chooses the active volcano as an adequate emblem for the energies seething within her. A deceptive silence, the apparent quiet of the volcano before it erupts, coincides with the poet's awareness of the absence of activity others see in her daily existence. Hers is "a still—Volcano—Life—" (poem 601) whose

---

²⁶ Hartman, "Wordsworth, Inscriptions, and Romantic Nature Poetry," p. 402.
²⁷ Wordsworth, "Salisbury Plain," 1. 44.
²⁸ *Ibid.*, 1. 158.

energy must be submerged, as a covering silence obscures the potential devastation of the power building within. Lost is the generative power of the landscape as well as its salutary effect. In its place Dickinson substitutes a vision of the poet whose responsibility is foremost the assertion of self against a threatening if evocative natural world.

IN *The Excursion,* Wordsworth's Wanderer tries to convince the Solitary to abandon his desperate solipsism, and this cautionary attempt suggests Wordsworth's own sense of solipsism's dangers. For him, the dream of nature serves as "an early, developmental step in converting the solipsistic into the sympathetic imagination: it entices the brooding soul out of itself, toward nature first, then toward humanity."[29] Dickinson, however, disrupts this process, for although she begins by observing nature and continues to write descriptive poems throughout her life, her most powerful poems perform a solipsistic usurpation of nature in which the imagination assumes complete control. Repeatedly Dickinson makes the distinction between the poem over which she exercises power and the natural world which retains its unpredictability. Dickinson's dismissal of a possible reconciliation with nature has, moreover, direct consequences upon her poems' structure. Whereas the Greater Romantic lyric resolves, in its tripartite structure, the conflict posed in its two initial movements, Dickinson either entirely omits this resolution or treats it ironically. Coleridge, rather than Wordsworth, provides the clearest instance for demonstrating Dickinson's use of this formalistic subversion.[30] Yet, the underlying reaction that her strategy articulates applies to the vision of both Precursor poets, their desire for and their

[29] Hartman, "Romanticism and 'Anti-Self-Consciousness,' " p. 55.

[30] This discussion of the formalistic relation between Dickinson's poem and Coleridge's depends upon M. H. Abrams' description of the major mode of the English Romantics, in his essay, "Structure and Style In the Greater Romantic Lyric," *From Sensibility to Romanticism.* eds. Frederick W. Hilles and Harold Bloom (Oxford: Oxford University Press, 1965). *N.B.*, pp. 527-528, 530-533, 538, 553-556.

Wordsworthian Nature

muted confidence in the possibility of achieving reciprocity with nature—a wedding of the natural world and the human imagination. Consider, for example, Dickinson's "The Frost was never seen—" in relation to Coleridge's "Frost at Midnight." In its closing lines, "Frost at Midnight" presents a harmonious image of the midnight winter scene illuminated by the radiant moon, a creative glow that reflects the process of the poet's imaginative movement from isolation to the companionship of self-created forms. The silent icicles reflecting the generative moonlight complete this vision of heartening feeling as the poem comes full circle into a calm reciprocity of light and human fulfillment. Dickinson's response to this poem reveals her attitude toward this benign image of reciprocal creativity, and shows, as well, her alternative conception of the relationship between nature and the imagination. First she takes the frost and fluttering flame, the two initially antithetical symbols of cold and warmth which fuse in Coleridge's poem, and transforms them into symbols of estrangement and destruction. She turns Coleridge's faith in the natural universe into anxiety, sacrificing the calm he experiences when musing upon the future through a reflection of the past. Dickinson transmutes Coleridge's night-vigil into a frustrated quest for answers denied her.

> The Frost was never seen—
> If met, too rapid passed,
> Or in too unsubstantial Team—
> The Flowers notice first
>
> A Stranger hovering round
> A Symptom of alarm
> In Villages remotely set
> But search effaces him
>
> Till some retrieveless Night
> Our Vigilance at waste
> The Garden gets the only shot
> That never could be traced.

> Unproved is much we know—
> Unknown the worst we fear—
> Of Strangers is the Earth the Inn
> Of Secrets is the Air—
>
> To analyze perhaps
> A Philip would prefer
> But Labor vaster than myself
> I find it to infer. (1202)

Coleridge's poem opens: "The Frost performs its secret ministry, / Unhelped by any wind." The frost, a productive, benign, natural force, pursues its religious task of forming icicles in silence. Dickinson responds: the frost evades one's attempts to view it; its presence is witnessed only by what it destroys. The secret of its process is the frustrated object of search for those who do not succumb to its lethal power. Experiencing her relationship to nature as one of fundamental estrangement, Dickinson telescopes Coleridge's stranger and the frost; her stranger is not the warmth within but the mysterious frost itself, which comes from a "village remotely set," a traveller presaging no companionable form but offering death, the symbol of expectancy converted to a "symptom of alarm." Whereas Coleridge's poem moves from the chill stillness of the outer world to the warmth of the fireside, Dickinson remains outside, contemplating the cold. Her search is futile as the frost escapes prying human eyes. The moment she puts down her guard, the frost damages her garden. This death takes the poem as far away from Coleridge's poem as it will go, and the reader suspects that Dickinson has deflected entirely from her source. But, just at this moment, she returns:

> Unproved is much we know—
> Unknown the worst we fear—
> Of Strangers is the Earth the Inn
> Of Secrets is the Air—

Wordsworthian Nature

The Strangers are all men who inhabit the earth, travellers in an alien, unforgiving land in which the atmosphere itself is charged with inescapable mystery. The secrets that bore Coleridge regenerative prophecies have become taunting enigmas which envelop all men. Dickinson raises her skeptical voice; she cannot analyze, as the disciple Philip had, the enigmas which confront her. She will not demand the proof he sought. She alludes, instead, as Johnson states in his note, to John 14: "Philip saith unto him, Lord, shew us the Father, and it sufficeth us. Jesus saith unto him, Have I been so long time with you, and yet hast thou not known me, Philip? he that hath seen me hath seen the Father; and how sayest thou then, Shew us the Father?" (98-99.) Dickinson uses the instance of the frost to illustrate the ignorance and doubt she experiences. Analysis will not suffice, for she has been robbed of the necessary energy which might allow her to "labor" unremittingly until she has either extracted knowledge from nature or admitted defeat. Instead, the poem's vision of destruction and defeat leaves her exhausted; she has vanquished any hope of rebuilding faith. A "stranger in a strange land," she is left only with the results of a nature she can neither pursue nor comprehend. Dickinson lapses into a lethargy destructive of creative thought, the opposite pole of imagination and the furthest possible psychological state from Coleridge's reassuring affirmation of the beneficent power of the universe. As Dickinson becomes increasingly estranged from nature, the elements in her landscape reveal only despair; and this isolation places a heavy burden on the poet that stops all creative activity, destroying as well the possibility of altering her own devastating vision.

The similarity of images, the echo of phrase, suggest that Dickinson had "Frost at Midnight" in mind when she conceived her poem. A comparison of these two poems suggests, furthermore, a pattern that emerges generally in Dickinson's relation to the Romantic poets. She seizes upon an image, a positive, creative vision, and transmutes it into her own vocabulary—one that reflects her sense of the painful division between the poet and nature; Dickinson finds death less an "easeful sleep" than a tormenting enigma, and internal quests become horrible nightmares. Although her attitudes are not uniform, the strategy of subversion remains constant. Formally as well as epistemologically, Dickinson severs the ties both Wordsworth and Coleridge thought essential to the health of modern man.

Yet, Wordsworth, fearing the implications of his own high claims for the imagination, fights what he surely sensed as the solipsistic dangers of his work. In Book IV of *The Excursion*, the Wanderer rebuts the despondent Solitary's argument by presenting an instance of restorative experience available to the man who remains open to nature. This generative experience is easiest for the child, whose relation to nature is more direct and unself-conscious. There are times, however, when the privileged reciprocity experienced by the child becomes available to the mature imagination:

> Even such a shell the universe itself
> Is to the ear of Faith; and there are times,
> I doubt not, when to you it doth impart
> Authentic tidings of invisible things; . . .[31]

Convolutions of pure reason devoid of an informing heart in communion with nature lead man toward destruction and despair. But nature will not fail the man who seeks to revive his once vivid childhood communion with the natural world. From this restorative experience, joy and a sense of righteousness arise—emotions which save man from falling into the despair that the Wanderer rejects. Dickinson comes closest to Wordsworth when she tries to read the meaning of light falling upon the land:

> There's a certain Slant of light,
> Winter Afternoons—
> That oppresses, like the Heft
> Of Cathedral Tunes—
> . . . . (258)

[31] Wordsworth, *The Excursion*, Bk. IV, ll. 1141-1144.

Wordsworthian Nature

Light, the element that bathes Wordsworth's landscapes, casts its shadow on this poem. The "certain slant" pierces the self, oppresses the spirit—it is not a seal of affirmation, but an "imperial affliction / Sent us of the Air." True to Wordsworthian *dicta*, Dickinson has responded to what she witnesses, but the light she finds is the type of doom she most fears. The "internal difference" filters down from Heaven through the landscape into the poet, and what for Wordsworth would be a reflective if sober moment becomes the "seal" of despair.

If Dickinson recalls Wordsworth, so he may approach her uncompromising vision, for instance in a poem from the group he named "Inscriptions." In "Written with a Slate Pencil on a Stone, on the Side of the Mountain of Black Comb," Wordsworth recounts the story of a "geographic Labourer," who had come to the mountain equipped to map the terrain and record "nature's process." Without warning, one day, his colorful map becomes invisible—darkness falls.

> As if the golden day itself had been
> Extinguished in a moment; total gloom,
> In which he sate alone, with unclosed eyes,
> Upon the blinded mountain's silent top![32]

The sudden eclipse baffles the geographer as it defies his authority. Nature asserts its domination over man's efforts to chart and measure "the grand terraqueous spectacle, / From centre to circumference, unveiled!"[33] which suddenly vanishes. Wordsworth ends the poem, leaving the geographer in darkness. He draws no enunciated moral nor does he preach the certainty of returning light. However, the experience that the poem recounts provides both moral and preachment. The inscription, written after the event, serves as warning for those beginning the climb up the mountain that nature is

---

[32] Wordsworth, "Written With A Slate Pencil On A Stone, On The Side of The Mountain of Black Comb," ll. 26-29.
[33] *Ibid.*, ll. 10-11.

indeed more formidable and mystifying than they may have assumed. The crisis of suddenly plunging into the unexplained darkness resembles Dickinson's perceptions of a nature rumbling with unpredictable volcanoes and wild bursts of lightning, which one can neither wholly understand nor control. The Inscription, in its function as warning, establishes the superiority of the poet over the scientific man. However, this superiority is limited, for the poet can warn of potential dangers only through his retrospective voice.

Dickinson shares in this evaluation of the relative merits of the strictly rational and intuitive approaches to natural process. "Split the lark and you'll find the music"[34] is only a single instance of Dickinson's delineating the results of those who "murder to dissect."[35] But the Wordsworthian "Inscription" bears another relation to Dickinson's work, for the two dominant conceptual terms she uses to describe her inner self and the imaginative possibilities of her thought are present in Wordsworth's poem. "Centre" and "circumference," which in Wordsworth's poem convey the limits of the globe that the geographer is attempting to survey, mean something characteristically different in Dickinson's vocabulary, as she applies these words not to the external world but to the core of her creative self and the extent to which her poetry can carry her. This is yet another instance of her radical internalization of metaphor from its place in landscape to the poetic consciousness.[36]

---

[34] Dickinson, Poem 861.

[35] Wordsworth, "The Tables Turned," 1. 28

[36] As I interpret Dickinson's use of the term, Circumference is the outermost extent the imagination can reach. The space thus created is what the self can explore, a kind of demarcation of imaginative limits and possibilities. When the circumference belongs to someone else, it signifies the boundaries of private experience:

> His mind of man, a secret makes
> I meet him with a start
> He carries a circumference
> In which I have no part

Wordsworthian Nature

By informing his view of reality with affective experience, Wordsworth creates a vision that is increasingly dependent upon human events to alter his relation to existence. The preeminent experience that educates the imagination is the death of someone particularly close, whose absence changes the poet's vision of the world. The affective experiences of the psyche necessarily alter one's view of the natural world, and grief provides the catalyst for this change. But whereas Wordsworth combines a lament for the lost freedom of his youth—an un-self-consciousness that did not hitherto question its own mortality—with a compensatory move toward a more humane vision, Dickinson admits no prior privileged condition:

> Must be a Wo—
> A loss or so—
> To bend the eye
> Best Beauty's way—
> . . . . (571)

"Wo" precedes the ability to perceive hidden beauty; to unlock the delight frozen within the stalactite, pain must be experienced. Ironically, "wo" creates the necessary slant that allows the eye to experience the difficulty of delight. Crucifixion precedes the bliss of revelation in poetry as well as religion: "Our lord—thought no / Extravagance / To pay— a Cross—." In this theory of aesthetic compensation, suffering yields an ability to witness beauty which depends directly upon the force of the pain. Wordsworth similarly acknowl-

---

Or even if I deem I do
He otherwise may know
Impregnable to inquest
However neighborly— (1663)

For an extended discussion of this notion of metaphor changed by Dickinson from an image that moves between the mind and nature to one dominated by the individuating characteristics of the imagination see Chapter Three. See also Robert Weisbuch's discussion of "anti-allegory" in *Emily Dickinson's Poetry* (Chicago: The University of Chicago Press, 1972), p. 48.

edges the difference such suffering makes to his vision of nature. In a poem to which Dickinson alludes in a letter, Wordsworth treats this relationship with death, the drowning of his brother, and the difference it made upon his perception of Peele Castle.[37] Although Wordsworth's claims for suffering are not so absolute as Dickinson's, his grief does reverse his former impression of the Castle as tranquil and serene. The perfect serenity of the poet's earlier experience has been transformed:

> So once it would have been,—'tis so no more;
> I have submitted to a new control:
> A power is gone, which nothing can restore;
> A deep distress hath humanised my Soul.[38]

Beaumont's painting of the tempestuous shore, "the lightning, the fierce wind, and trampling waves," seems, after the poet's grief, an accurate portrayal of the shore he had once viewed with such remote tranquillity.[39] Wordsworth laments his former self:

> Farewell, farewell the heart that lives alone,
> Housed in a dream, at distance from the Kind![40]

His earlier, happy heart was innocent of the realities of human suffering and consequently blind.

As for Dickinson, it has taken a "wo" to provide Wordsworth with a different vision of life. This altered perception *reflects the sublimity of existence—a dark, tumultuous scene* which makes his original version of castle and shore pale in comparison. Along with this new vision, however, Words-

---

[37] For Dickinson's allusion to this poem, see letter no. 315, II, 449 and letter no. 394, II, 510.

[38] Wordsworth's "Elegiac Stanzas, suggested by a Picture of Peele Castle, in a Storm, painted by Sir George Beaumont," 11. 33-36.

[39] Wordsworth, "Elegiac Stanzas," 1. 52

[40] *Ibid.*, 11. 53-54.

worth recognizes the loss of the bold power of innocence, the untroubled energy of one spared the knowledge of his mortality. But Dickinson derives a different benefit from her grief, one consistent with the distinction we have been drawing between her sensibility and Wordsworth's. For her, "wo" precedes the only vision she acknowledges: that which emphasizes absence, loss, or renunciation. She does not record the former freedom Wordsworth laments; for her, the sources of strength are tapped from an essential grief.

Strategies for coping with such loss draw Wordsworth and Dickinson closer, for both invoke the sheer staying power of the self as it endures as well as embodies what most threatens it and what it most fears:

> When I hoped I feared—
> Since I hoped I dared
> Everywhere alone
> As a Church remain—
> Spectre cannot harm—
> Serpent cannot charm—
> He deposes Doom
> Who hath suffered him—(1181)

In his "Elegiac Stanzas, suggested by a Picture of Peele Castle," Wordsworth evokes a related power—the dignity of a fortress in a storm. Donald Wesling, in his *Wordsworth and the Adequacy of Landscape*, comments on the poet's description of the building: "Peele Castle itself as the leading subject is described in a dense quatrain as presenting the stoic defensive alternative; the castle becomes one of the noblest of the unspeaking solitaries."[41] The stanza to which Wesling refers evokes the presence of ". . . this huge Castle, standing here sublime," which Wordsworth admires. "I love to see the look with which it braves, / Cased in the unfeeling armour

---

[41] Donald Wesling, *Wordsworth and the Adequacy of Landscape* (New York: Barnes & Noble, Inc., 1970), p. 51.

of old time, / The lightning, the fierce wind, and trampling waves."[42] Exposure and seclusion are combined in the heroic image of consciousness as fortress. "Wordsworth," Wesling goes on to explain, "draws on writers like Burke and Alison for his notion that enduring objects are properly sublime, but he presses further than they do, in his belief that sublimity can be an attribute of the suffering human mind when it braves its appropriate terrors with only the armour of accumulated experience."[43]

DICKINSON shares Wordsworth's sense of the sublimity of the suffering human mind; but she, as does Wordsworth, goes beyond her predecessor to assert that the human imagination is the initial source of this sublimity and that nature, un-self-conscious and necessarily unaware, is not the source but the reflection of the stoicism within the human observer. The strength of the Dickinsonian self only increases as the burden grows heavier.

> . . . .
> Power is only Pain—
> Stranded, thro' Discipline,
> Till Weights—will hang—
> Give Balm—to Giants—
> And they'll wilt, like Men—
> Give Himmaleh—
> They'll Carry—Him! (252)

The mind has its own terrain; ideas and emotions assume solid forms in this interior space. The physical properties of weight, balance, and structure apply to the process of consciousness. Stones lie at the bottom of the mind which crush what judgment rejects:

> It dropped so low—in my Regard—
> I heard it hit the Ground—

---

[42] Wordsworth, "Elegiac Stanzas," ll. 49-51.
[43] Wesling, p. 59.

> And go to pieces on the Stones
> At bottom of my Mind—
>
> Yet blamed the Fate that fractured—*less*
> Than I reviled Myself,
> For entertaining Plated Wares
> Upon my Silver Shelf— (747)

The self, interior space, provides the ultimate test for any experience, or person outside it. The individual has become sole arbiter of existence; thus the self must receive constant scrutiny so that it can be strengthened and preserved.

This consolidation of power into the individual imagination results in nature's relinquishing its commemorative or votive functions. The only memorial that can be trusted is inscribed on the self:

> After a hundred years
> Nobody knows the Place
> Agony that enacted there
> Motionless as Peace
>
> Weeds triumphant ranged
> Strangers strolled and spelled
> At the lone Orthography
> Of the Elder Dead
>
> Winds of Summer Fields
> Recollect the way—
> Instinct picking up the Key
> Dropped by memory— (1147)

The site of the grave no longer calls to the traveller; the place has lost its function in the landscape. Winds, invisible and shifting, remember the way to the home of the final agony and assume a significance greater than the weed-covered stone.[44] A mingling of instinct and memory leads one to this

---

[44] Discussing the role of the wind in Dickinson's poetry, Northrop Frye identifies it with the Holy Spirit, the "giver of life to nature and of inspi-

stone covered with "triumphant," because disguising, weeds. The process of stone calling to stranger is broken—the stone hidden, its inscription a mystery. People walk casually around the graves, "strolling" among the tombstones. By using "orthography," Dickinson insists upon the loss of meaning in the inscriptions carved above the graves. And such reinforcement of the emphasis on individual letters devoid of coherence contributes further to the impotence of the inscriptions. Only the sincerity of unabashed human affection can insure the permanence of any monument. Echoing Horace, to revise his meaning, Dickinson writes:

> An honest Tear
> Is durabler than Bronze—
> This Cenotaph
> May each that dies—
>
> Reared by itself—
> No Deputy suffice—
> Gratitude bears
> When Obelisk decays (1192)

Here is Horace:

> *Exegi monumentum aere perennius*
> *regalique situ pyramidum altius,*
> *quod non imber edax, non Aquilo impotens*
> *possit diruere aut innumerabilis*
> *annorum series et fuga temporum.*

Dickinson shifts the Horation comparison from ode and artifact to unmediated emotion and physical memorial.[45] Without the spontaneous, honest tear, the cenotaph is devoid of

---

ration to humanity, the creative force that makes the poet's verses 'breathe,' and the 'Conscious Ear' that imagination hears with." (*Fables of Identity: Studies in Poetic Identity* [New York: Harcourt, Brace & World, Inc., 1963]), p. 210.

[45] The translation reads:

meaning. The single tear endows the monument with the only significance it can possess. Consequently, Dickinson deprives the memorial of its function to recall the presence of the dead to the living; for her such a role is purely gratuitous.

However, the stone does serve other purposes as the terms of the relationship between visitor, monument, and memorialized shift. If those who remain have forgotten the dead, the tombstone becomes a chiding reminder that they have belied the trust placed in them by those who have died. The external object, once again, serves as a taunting spur to guilt.

> She laid her docile Crescent down
> And this confiding Stone
> Still states to Dates that have forgot
> The News that she is gone—
>
> So constant to it's stolid trust,
> The Shaft that never knew—
> It shames the Constancy that fled
> Before it's emblem flew— (1396)

The unconscious and unfeeling shaft shames those no longer faithful. The "confiding" stone can tell the dates of birth and death, but no more. The "Constancy" of the stone refers exclusively to its actual presence, ironically implying its inability to be anything other than stationary; it is constant to a *stolid* trust—unemotional and unresponsive. But even this most primitive and mute memorial can serve as a rebuke to the people who should be the source of its meaning and power. They have failed the stone just as they failed the per-

---

> More durable than bronze, higher than Pharaoh's
> Pyramids is the monument I have made,
> A shape that angry wind or hungry rain
> Cannot demolish, nor the innumerable
> Ranks of the years that march in centuries.

Horace, XXX, Book III, *Odes* in *The Odes of Horace*, trans. James Michie (New York: Washington Square Press, 1965), pp. 202-203.

son who lies beneath it. The "emblem" refers both to the actual inscription and to the person behind the name. The packed diction of the poem's last two lines points in different directions: first, it suggests that the stolid, inchoate stone is a source of shame to those who have abandoned the memory of the dead; and, secondly, that the emblem, the inscription, has fled in the wake of the departing life that is now forgotten. The inscription derives its sole significance from its relation to the life to which it refers. The failure of the living to remember the dead nullifies the votive power of the stone and changes it instead into an object that provokes their sense of guilt. The power of the stone depends directly on the consciousness of others. "Death sets a Thing significant"; it imbues the possessions of the deceased with renewed human associations. Death itself, therefore, becomes the bond between object and person which lends the relic meaning.

One need not, however, remain simply the recipient of such powerful gifts, for, according to Dickinson, it is the primary function of the poet to wrest from the passing moment its life and raise it above time, beyond death.[46] In a poem which itself speaks as an unnamed epitaph, she describes what it means to be a poet:

> This was a Poet—It is That
> Distills amazing sense

---

[46] In her recent book, *Wordsworth: Language As Counter-Spirit* (New Haven: Yale University Press, 1977), Frances Ferguson describes the significance of the epitaphic model for Wordsworth's ideas of language: "By placing the funeral monument rather than passionate utterance at the beginning of his version of language, Wordsworth establishes the sign of mortality at the origin of language, so that the incarnation of language always seems to involve a gesture not merely towards the feelings which precede language but also towards the disembodied state of immortality which no longer has need of language" (p. 33).

In Dickinson's poems, the emphasis on the funeral monument is also very much in evidence; however, this "disembodied state of immortality" is the place she wishes her language to penetrate. "Immortality," as she once stated, was her "Flood subject" and through language, she kept trying to bridge the space between the living and the dead.

Wordsworthian Nature

From ordinary Meanings—
And Attar so immense

From the familiar species
That perished by the Door—
We wonder it was not Ourselves
Arrested it—before—

Of Pictures, the Discloser—
The Poet—it is He—
Entitles Us—by Contrast—
To ceaseless Poverty—

Of Portion—so unconscious—
The Robbing—could not harm—
Himself—to Him—a Fortune—
Exterior—to Time— (448)

To be "Exterior—to Time"—this is the aim of Dickinson's poems. And they themselves can be seen as a kind of epitaphic monument, brief forms that are not fragmentary but take the shape of inscriptions constructed with a granitic craftsmanship that arrests the eye and coerces the reader to pause and remember. One of language's primary functions is to salvage momentary experience from its place in the natural world and preserve it from death. This conception of poem as evocative monument remains a useful image only so long as it can work upon the reader. When it fails to elicit a response, the power of the word itself comes into question. Because Dickinson can trust neither the world nor another to provide solace or inspiration, the success or failure of her poems assumes an extraordinary importance. What can success or failure mean; how can it be measured for a poet who did not publish her work? Or did she have in mind the creation of a monument to experience, which only those who came after her would read and preserve?

In her characteristically oblique way, Dickinson suggests an answer to these speculations: there is one ear she wishes to reach. And if she fails, all else might be forgotten. Frustrated by the silence of this single other, Dickinson adopts a monumental symbol of ancient, mythic powers to express the terms of her predicament. She chooses the Memnon Stone to symbolize the mysterious presence from whom she hopes to win a response:

> Put up my lute!
> What of—my Music!
> Since the sole ear I cared to charm—
> Passive—as Granite—laps My Music—
> Sobbing—will suit—as well as psalm!
>
> Would but the 'Memnon' of the Desert—
> Teach me the strain
> That vanquished Him—
> When He—surrendered to the Sunrise—
> Maybe—that—would awaken—them! (261)

Unable to bewitch the one for whom it was intended, her music falls unheeded, like lapping waves on smooth stone. Whereas Wordsworth conceives of a marriage between nature and self, between mutually reinforcing powers as the ego and the land meet, Dickinson envisions a contest in which she, as outsider, must either seize or renounce the forces on which she fears she must rely. Dickinson desires Memnon's secret; she wishes to learn the strain which could so move him that, from the dry earth of silence, his voice would rise in a correspondingly affirmative song. The words "surrendered" and "vanquished" strengthen the aura of aggressive intimacy between the Singer and Memnon, the lover and her beloved adversary, the poet and her silent muse. Towering Memnon is the keeper of secret power, for he holds the knowledge Dickinson desires in order to make her poems live in and through another. What she continuously fears is this other's absence, silence, or withdrawal of support. Because he alone has such power, his role as judge assigns him a place of overwhelming importance in her creative process. Without a corresponding voice, the poet sings alone, and since her stated intent is to communicate, her song becomes worthless and might just as well be abandoned.

In "Put up my lute," Dickinson signals the failure of her godlike lover to voice his approval, to welcome her song. The unresponsiveness of another's voice joins with the inaccessibility she fears in her Calvinist God, and the dangers of an inviolate nature to threaten her relationship to everything outside the self. Yet, despite such repeated disappointments, the poems keep asserting the need to break past the constraints of silence and compel a response. In her boldest attempt to overcome these constraints, Dickinson strives to find a voice that will carry her between the living and the dead. With this gesture, her poems assume the functions of epitaphs and invocations, chiselled words that attempt to revive faded meanings, propitiating words spoken in the face of the final silence of death. No longer able to trust in the consolation Wordsworth addresses, afraid of a nature he sought to view as potentially benign, Dickinson writes epitaphs that revive the memory and extend momentary experience within the life of the poem. For both poets, the power associated with the act of writing depends upon the ability of that act to wrest from death its intimidating silence, to create a province of language that remains impervious even to the threat of death itself.

III

Keats, Dickinson, and the Poet's Romance

> Their words are chosen out of their desire,
> The joy of language, when it is themselves.
> —Wallace Stevens

POETIC AUTONOMY is not bestowed freely upon a poet but must be won by the skills of the imagination. Dickinson's quest for independence, as I have been suggesting, diverges in crucial ways from the Romantics' relationship of poet and muse. Her quest is not, however, so much a rejection of their vision of the heroic poet as it is a reassessment of the relationship of poet to muse based upon the fact that a woman is now at the center of the creative endeavor. In her vision of the analogue between the origins of creativity and the paradigms of romantic (and Romantic) love, Dickinson most closely resembles Keats; yet even as she shares with him the erotic trope for poetic creation, she distinguishes her vision of *eros* from his in ways that clarify her relationship to the Romantic imagination and her subversion of its underlying assumptions. Although she may adopt the language of Romanticism, Dickinson separates herself from its aspirations by rejecting the possibilities of a benign reciprocity not only between self and world but between self and those forces which she deems outside it, be they other poets or projections of internal energies that she cannot recognize as her own. Nevertheless, as with the Romantics, the tension between self and other, the attempts to resolve this dichotomy, remain among her foremost concerns.

Dickinson is not alone, however, in her questioning of Wordsworth's salutary vision of the power of landscape to

The Poet's Romance

speak to the inquiring poet. In his sonnet "To Ailsa Rock," Keats witnesses the same silence Dickinson so often decries.[1] He asks the rock to reveal its origins, the tumult of history which rests within its silence:[2]

> Thou answer'st not; for thou art dead asleep;
>   Thy life is but two dead eternities—
> The last in air, the former in the deep;[3]

But this is Keats addressing a fact of nature; he comes even closer to Dickinson when he asks the inspiriting force of poetry itself to

> Read me a lesson, Muse, and speak it loud
> Upon the top of Nevis, blind in mist![4]

Desiring the secrets of nature shrouded from man by mist, he pleads for knowledge. What he discovers is that his feet are standing on "craggy stones."[5] He learns no more of heaven, hell, or earth, and his frustrated appeal foreshadows Dickinson's own desire to wrench from nature the "truth" that lies hidden beyond appearance. Keats's need for another, his call for an answering voice, rises from the erotic analogue he draws between Romantic love and the working mind, for he portrays the creative act as a process based on a relationship of sexual power. Poetry exists in the same realm as love, an erotic paradigm that fuses instinct and high imagination.

Keats's heroes (in such poems as *Endymion*, "La Belle Dame Sans Merci" and "Lamia") fall in love with or seek to woo goddesses. The relation between the mortal lover and his

---

[1] See, for example, Emily Dickinson, Poem 261, line 4, 187.

[2] Dickinson describes the "sole ear" that comprises her audience as "granite." (See Poem 261, line 4.)

[3] John Keats, "To Ailsa Rock," *The Poems of John Keats*, ed. H. W. Garrod (London: Oxford University Press, 1966), 11. 9-10. This edition of Keats's poems is used throughout the chapter.

[4] Keats, "Read me a lesson, Muse, and speak it loud," 11. 1-2.

[5] *Ibid.*, 1. 10.

unearthly, exotic beloved is perilously unequal and marked with dangers. The mortal hero, the poet, cannot comprehend his goddess; he suffers because of his own essentially limited human identity. Both Mnemosyne in *Hyperion* and Moneta in *The Fall of Hyperion: A Fragment* are otherworldly, mysterious figures who have the power to destroy or redeem the suppliant poet-god standing before them. Keats's relation to the eternal female, the erotic other, is charged with apprehension and determined by the imbalance of the poet and his Muse. She resembles the recurring persona in Dickinson's poems whom she called the Stranger, a presence that has the power to determine the fate of the searching, mortal poet by rejecting or fulfilling her plea for inspiration and approval. In *Hyperion*, Apollo realizes that he owes his lyre to Mnemosyne, who has been both guardian and inspiriting force. Apollo stands, eyes sealed, "in aching ignorance" before the source of his power; he neither knows the reason for his crisis nor can he escape it.[6] At first, he cannot even recall Mnemosyne's name, but must ask, "Where is power," and read the lesson of the mute goddess from her face.[7] Knowledge "pour[s] into the wide hollows" of his brain; infused with her meaning, he dies into life.[8]

So, in *The Fall of Hyperion*, Keats faces what Robert Gittings characterizes as that "terrifying female figure" who wields over the poet the power of life and death.[9] Parting the veils surrounding Moneta, the poet uncovers

> . . . a wan face,
> Not pin'd by human sorrows, but bright-blanch'd
> by an immortal sickness which kills not;
> It works a constant change, which happy death
> Can put no end to; deathwards progressing
> To no death was that visage; it had past
> The lilly and the snow; and beyond these

[6] Keats, *Hyperion*, III, 1. 107.   [7] *Ibid.*, 1. 103.
[8] *Ibid.*, 1. 117.
[9] Robert Gittings, *John Keats: The Living Year* (Cambridge: Harvard University Press, 1954), p. 179.

The Poet's Romance

> I must not think now, though I saw that face—
> But for her eyes I should have fled away.[10]

So mysterious and pathetic was that wan face that even in recollection the poet cannot bear to dwell on it for more than a moment. Moneta, a veiled image evoking pity and awe, finally yields to Keats's desire to know. However, the sinuous Lamia—goddess, snake, and female form—remains a threat; she leads Lycius to his death, a process in which he abandons his pursuit of objective, rational knowledge to the passion of love.[11] In *La Belle Dame*, another female shrouded in mystery leaves the knight she has wooed wandering forlorn and pale upon the desolate hillside. Each of these female emanations possesses mystery, impenetrability, and a lethal potency. Keats's relation to this female form is defined by his hungering for a union that the dangerous woman-goddess views with reluctance or rejects. This Female assumes either of two dominant forms—the untouchable, remote, statuesque "mother" or the provocative, earthy, protean nymph, but neither allows an equable relationship within the possibilities of any mortal man.

Keats does, however, embrace such a balanced vision in his "Ode to Psyche." Here he finds a blissful, satisfying love, one that allows him to create the privileged ground of conception where he presides as naturalistic priest. He wins for the "winged Psyche" an immutable garden of infinite variety, what Dickinson elsewhere calls the "Blossom of the Brain."[12] This benign vision depends upon the power of the triumphant imagination's using its force to create a place where the limits of mortal love fall away. The poet creates extra-natural flowers and "stars without a name," unknown to the outside world because they are formed by Fancy, the

---

[10] Keats, *The Fall of Hyperion: A Dream*, Canto I, ll. 256-64.

[11] Garrett Stewart, in his essay "*Lamia* and the Language of Metamorphosis" (*Studies in Romanticism*, Vol. 15, No. 1, Winter 1976, 3-41) remarks on Lamia's "many-faceted, baroquely discrepant loveliness" (p. 11) and suggests that "she seems to stand in and for the mortal flux." (p. 37).

[12] Dickinson, Poem 945, l. 1.

agent of the active imagination.[13] Each unnamed poem is a singular emanation, an immortal result of the poet's art:

> And there shall be for thee all soft delight
>   That shadowy thought can win,
> A bright torch, and a casement ope at night,
>   To let the warm Love in![14]

Even in this most luxuriant and hopeful vision, the love the poet desires to welcome rests in the future, for the image is a projected rather than an achieved reality. Yet what Keats wins here is an active wooing on behalf of the poet coupled with a welcoming receptivity. The analogue of Cupid and Psyche to the Poet and his Muse is clear: the poet courts his *feminine image* with his "tuneless numbers"; the Ode itself is the preeminent creation of the gardener of the imagination.[15] He woos Psyche with her own words as he sings to her with the voice of love:

> And pardon that thy secrets should be sung
> Even into thine own soft-conched ear,[16]

Keats, however, wishes to serve not only Psyche but Cupid as well. Though he worships the goddess who has arrived "too late for antique vows" and "fond believing lyre,"[17] he also exalts the power of his own vision of the "two fair creatures, couched side by side / In deepest grass."[18] By appropriating the external symbols of worship into the self, he is determined to become Psyche's priest, poet, and home. Darkness and secrecy, the disguise of night and the possibility of distrust (the conditions of the myth of Apuleius) give way to an alternative landscape bathed in light and open to the freedom of love.[19]

[13] Keats, "Ode to Psyche," 1. 61.
[14] *Ibid.*, 11. 64-67.
[15] *Ibid.*, 1. 1.
[16] *Ibid.*, 11. 3-4.
[17] *Ibid.*, 1. 37.
[18] *Ibid.*, 11. 9-10.
[19] Douglas Bush writes: "The poem does not embody the traditional allegory of Cupid and Psyche." (*Mythology and the Romantic Tradition in English*

The Poet's Romance

Echoing the generative metaphor of garden and developing seed, Dickinson asserts an equal claim for the powers of the imagination, but she removes the lovers from the internal landscape.

> This is a Blossom of the Brain—
> A small—italic Seed
> Lodged by Design or Happening
> The Spirit fructified—
> . . . . (945)

Dickinson's blossom is rare, the process of its creation a mystery. Keats's refulgent garden, bathed in light and proffering a welcome to the mythic lovers, contrasts with Dickinson's signal flower, "A small—italic Seed." The scarcity and mystery of this "Blossom of the Brain" enhance its value as its loss marks the death of God. The window which stood open to "let the warm love in" has been closed; the origin of creation protects its sources, barring future intimacy. The initial steps in building the sacred place are taken alone, for Dickinson relies on no one to lay the foundation—she remains master and sole craftsman of her art:

> Myself was formed—a Carpenter—
> An unpretending time
> My Plane—and I, together wrought
> Before a Builder came—
>
> To measure our attainments—
> Had we the Art of Boards

Poetry [New York: Norton, 1963], p. 106.) However, I sense deliberate inverted echoes of Apuleius in the closing lines of the "Ode" when Keats draws a distinct comparison between the sanctuary he has created in his imagination to the locus of the myth. The torch, instead of burning Cupid's shoulder, proffers him a guide to the chamber; the brightness of the "room" maintains its superiority over the meeting place of the mythic Cupid and Psyche who had to greet one another in darkness lest the identity of Cupid be discovered by his lover. Keats offers a superior realm, freed from the constraints of necessary deception and the pain of betrayal.

The Poet's Romance

> Sufficiently developed—He'd hire us
> At Halves—
>
> My Tools took Human—Faces—
> The Bench, where we had toiled—
> Against the Man—persuaded—
> We—Temples build—I said— (488)

Refusing to relinquish her independence to the authority of another, Dickinson builds "temples" that deny external limitations or the intruding "master." Thus, natural process is suspended, usurped by the poetic imagination's ability to construct an alternative time and space. Defined by her solitary consciousness, this new time repudiates the possibility of loss by denying the inevitability of change. The sanctity of Dickinson's inner garden corresponds to Keats's privileged ground, for it is only within the self-created landscape that love can win freedom from anxiety and the fear of death.[20]

The benign, projected vision of the "Ode to Psyche" allows Keats the power to serve his commitment to an ideal love. Rarely, however, is his vision of love so free from anxiety as it is here. Once the poet actually confronts the goddess, he is threatened; and too often he finds himself waiting in vain or pursuing the impossible. Crucial to the beneficent aura of the "Ode to Psyche" is the poet's androgynous freedom, for he associates himself both with the activity of the masculine lover and with the receptivity of his beloved. Pervading this sexual coupling is the asexual image of the priest, the celebrant who constructs a sacramental region for the lovers. The evocative moan of the choir at midnight and the teeming incense fill the poem with a sensuality which Keats does not restrict to male or female. Instead, this mystical luxuriance cloaks priest, garden, and celebrant alike. The garden of the imagination holds within it both male and female as Keats invites the form of love and its desire, Eros

---

[20] Dickinson, Poem 500, l. 15.

The Poet's Romance

and Psyche, to enter the rosy sanctuary within the "wide quietness" of his mind.[21] But the beneficent vision of this ode is a rare achievement. More often the female form is split from him; and the poet introjects the benign, receptive powers of the female self, leaving the destructive, awesome image of the feminine to inhabit his projections. Commenting on one of these lethal female forms, Douglas Bush quotes John Middleton Murry: "The truth about the Lamia . . . is that Keats himself did not know whether she was a thing of beauty or a thing of bale. He only knew that if he were to be deprived of her, he would die, which he did, in the poem and in fact."[22] However, Keats is bound to this threatening form by a need to possess her regardless of the sacrifice. In "La Belle Dame" the pale knight can neither be sustained on the roots and manna the goddess provides for him nor can he survive without her—she has him in "thrall."

The identity of this powerful, protean, feminine other—possessor of hidden knowledge and fatal charms—joins in Keats's mind with the figure of the muse and poetry itself. And it is poetry that becomes the occasion for an erotic intensity denied by life as well as by the domineering female image. Writing to his friend Benjamin Bailey, Keats states: "The Imagination may be compared to Adam's dream—he awoke and found it truth."[23] What Adam found when he awoke was woman, the fulfillment of an oneiric slumber that granted him the companionship of another human form. The Imagination engenders a distinct, antithetical reality: the creation of the feminine form out of the marrow of the masculine self. The midwife of dreams bears a part of Adam into a life that offers the possibility of love as well as temptation. Freed through sleep, the active imagination creates a new antithetical self. Clearly, Keats sees the powerful imagination in terms of the procreative process resulting from the union

---

[21] Keats, "Ode to Psyche," 1. 58.

[22] Bush, *Mythology and the Romantic Tradition*, p. 112.

[23] John Keats, *The Letters*, ed. Hyder Edward Rollins (Cambridge: Harvard University Press, 1958), letter no. 43, I, 185, November 22, 1817, to Benjamin Bailey. See also Milton's *Paradise Lost*, VIII, 11. 436-500.

of Adam and Eve. In an earlier letter, he recalls reading Spenser's lines in the *Faerie Queene*:

> 'The Noble Heart that harbors vertuous thought,
> And is with Child of glorious great intent,
> Can never rest, until it forth have brought
> Th' eternal Brood of Glory excellent—'[24]

The child-bearing heart finds its companion in the Apollo's head which "is pregnant with poetic lore"; male and female reside and create within the single self.[25] Poetry is a lady to be won, the object of a dangerous yet essential flirtation.[26] Keats muses, "I know not why Poetry and I have been so distant lately I must make some advances soon or she will cut me entirely."[27] And in a dark mood, Keats "confounds poetry, death, and love."[28] Mario D'Avanzo, in his *Keats's Metaphors for the Poetic Imagination*, sums up his discussion of the relation of woman and poetry by suggesting that Keats felt:

"The more intense the poet's perception of the object of beauty—and we have established that for Keats a woman is the supreme embodiment of beauty—the more stimulated is his sympathetic imagination through the most intense form of sensory experience, sexual love. The 'chameleon poet' completely loses his 'self' and is elevated to the heights of imaginative activity. The sexual act in Keats's poems therefore figures the ultimate imaginative intensity and is consequently 'creative of essential beauty.' The frenzied creative

---

[24] Keats, *Letters*, letter no. 22, I, 134, 17, 18 April 1817, to J. H. Reynolds. *The Faerie Queene*, I.v.i.

[25] Keats, *Letters*, letter no. 5, I, 106, August 1816, to George Keats.

[26] Mario D'Avanzo (*Keats's Metaphors for the Poetic Imagination* [Durham, N.C.: Duke University Press, 1967]) has discovered several instances of Keats's use of the paradigm of sexual love and the image of the feminine when he writes of the imagination and the "demon Poesy." See D'Avanzo, p. 49.

[27] Keats, *Letters*, letter no. 159, II, 74, 13 March 1819, to the George Keatses.

[28] Keats, *Letters*, I, 370, cited by D'Avanzo, p. 25.

art of the poet finds its fit analogue in sexual union, where the woman, playing the part of the imagination *conceives*, bestowing her knowledge upon the aroused poet at the supreme moment. . . ."[29]

This is indeed the ideal Keatsian vision when all anxiety melts away under the pressure of the "chief intensity."[30] But the supreme moment is surrounded by a past and a future. Within the compass of a larger, extensive reality, the female, that "supreme embodiment of beauty," becomes an image of dread power and awesome potency. And it is this image of the feminine "other" that again recalls Dickinson's Stranger.

The masculine erotic "other" in Dickinson serves a generative function as source and occasion for her poems; a figure of astounding authority, it is he to whom she owes her existence. She lives as if he listens; the internal adversary becomes her sole audience:

> All that I do
> Is in review
> To his enamored mind
> I know his eye
> Where e'er I ply
> Is pushing close behind
>
> Not any Port
> Nor any flight
> But he doth there preside
> What omnipresence lies in wait
> For her to be a Bride (1496)

The ominous echo of approaching death merges with the omnipresent image of the lover, a fusion that betrays an anxiety that has its sources in the fear of mortality. Yet this same hovering presence offers the promise of creativity as well as the threat of dissolution. And this essentially oxymoronic image embodies Dickinson's wildly ambivalent perception

[29] D'Avanzo, p. 36.
[30] Keats, *Endymion*, I, 1. 800.

The Poet's Romance

of her mythic poet-lover. She insists upon the identity of poetry and love, yet the climactic moment brings with it assured destruction:

> To pile like Thunder to it's close
> Then crumble grand away
> While Everything created hid
> This—would be Poetry—
>
> Or Love—the two coeval come—
> We both and neither prove—
> Experience either and consume—
> For None see God and live— (1247)

The exaltation of the first stanza vies with the threat of the closing lines of the poem as her vision of the sublime awe of echoing thunder conveys her cosmic ambition.[31] Just as she wishes her mouth to spill forth hot lava—the rushing rock which would silence all others—so in this poem Dickinson would send all nature into hiding with the sound of her voice magnified throughout creation. The climactic moment followed by distant rumblings is her definition of poetry—destructive and magnificent at once. Love builds with poetry to an overwhelming force, but neither can be subjected to

[31] Anderson (*Emily Dickinson's Poetry: Stairway of Surprise*) discusses this poem:

"All too frequently her force does explode, as in the poem under consideration. To express oneself like a thunderbolt, 'This—would be Poetry' she had begun. But in the end this powerful figure is replaced by that of fire, the burning bush; such a poet would 'consume' himself, 'For None see God and live.' Elsewhere, in reworking the Biblical account of God's apparition on Mount Sinai, she discounts Moses' boast as an improbable fable, declaring 'No man saw awe.' Out of the fragments of these poems some interesting links can be made. The poetic experience is equated with religious awe, so that the ultimate perception would be like seeing God. But this is impossible, and the poet can only hope to catch a glimpse and record it in earthly forms before he is consumed. Fire and ice, volcanoes, thunder and lightning—only the most violent images drawn from nature seemed adequate for the intensities that compelled her to expression. She had moved a long way in both theory and practice from the ideal of emotion recollected in tranquility" (pp. 72-73).

proof, for they exist beyond the pursuit of certainty. Experiencing either ensures personal destruction; having equated love and poetry with God, she asserts that they require the same complete sacrifice. As one cannot see God and live, one cannot experience the equal power of love or poetry and expect to survive. The occasion for exultation is necessarily the same experience which engenders destruction. The climax of love and its coevals provokes fear, for the natural world seeks protection from the magisterial, threatening power that descends from the sky.[32] Such a moment of annunciation breaks through mortality to create an altered condition which marks an irrevocable change. Dickinson's perception of love and poetry as equivalent to the soul's confrontation with God emphasizes the threshold of experience, a moment of liminal awareness when "All—is the price of All—".[33]

This identification of love, poetry, and revelation reflects Dickinson's hierarchy, which identifies these three liminal experiences as the supreme moments of existence. She "probes retrieveless things" and pays just the price of life for her achievement.[34] The poet-stranger-lover vies with Dickinson in this field of myth. And, conscious of the mythic quality of her war, its perpetual reenactment, its cyclic victory and defeat, Dickinson acknowledges the need for a continual joining of foes to make a poem. Thus psychic pauses assume the shape of poems—brief evocations which mark moments of triumph, despair, or stasis—a heightened awareness produced by the embattled imagination as it faces its antithetical self.

> We dream—it is good we are dreaming—
> It would hurt us—were we awake—
> But since it is playing—kill us,
> And we are playing—shriek—
>
> What harm? Men die—externally—
> It is a truth—of Blood—

---

[32] For a discussion of this poem in terms of its images, see pp. 126 ff.
[33] Dickinson, Poem 772.   [34] Dickinson, Poem 532.

The Poet's Romance

> But we—are dying in Drama—
> And Drama—is never dead—
>
> Cautious—We jar each other—
> And either—open the eyes—
> Lest the Phantasm—prove the Mistake—
> And the livid Surprise
>
> Cool us to Shafts of Granite—
> With just an Age—and Name—
> And perhaps a phrase in Egyptian—
> It's prudenter—to dream— (531)

The lethal finality of the external cannot intrude upon this drama of love, poetry, and dream. Absolute "proof" implies death, a passing beyond the liminal moment into a silent, irrevocable oblivion. Her "play," a ritual of blood, becomes bearable only in this condition of oneiric semi-consciousness. Ironically, just because it is a mythic drama, the stakes are total, the injuries internal. And the controlling irony of the poem depends upon the fact of "play" being fused with the destructive potency of the players. The illusion of the game must be preserved, the psychic delusion sustained lest the cycle break into the physical reality of death. Thus the dream is a precondition for Dickinson's psychic war; she wills an essential blindness agreed upon by the mutual consent of self and other so that the myth may continue and the self survive.

The struggle of the "dream" enacts Dickinson's ambivalence toward her essential adversary, an ambivalence that extends beyond Keats's coupling of pleasure and sorrow. Whereas his acceptance, the fullness of his humanistic vision, depends upon a sustained awareness of the beauty of life and the imminence of loss, Dickinson releases the tension implicit in this simultaneity of opposites.[35] Rather than ac-

---

[35] As Cynthia describes this condition:
> 'Endymion: woe! woe! is grief contain'd
> In the very deeps of pleasure, my sole life?'—
> (*Endymion*, II, 823-824)

The Poet's Romance

knowledge the necessity of pain within joy, she sees reality through the eyes of one conversant with Original Sin. Pain becomes the price one must pay for joy—a compensatory sacrifice subsumes the possibility of happiness. Her perception of the compensatory nature of life differs fundamentally from Keats's oxymoronic view because she attends to the cost required by existence while Keats moves toward an acceptance that belies the need for the stern balance of accounts she insists upon. Dickinson never forgets one cannot have the pleasure without the pain, or the satisfaction and the longing. So she opts for longing, a condition of constant deprivation that imparts the intensity of experience more vividly than the dulled memory of the fulfilled.

This recourse to the "negative way" also characterizes Dickinson's relationships with the ubiquitous, internal, masculine other. Once he enters her life, his presence persists, and his critical ear assumes dominance. A reciprocal mutuality remains in the distance, an enviable but impossible condition.

> I rose—because He sank—
> I thought it would be opposite—
> But when his power dropped—
> My Soul grew straight.
>
> I cheered my fainting Prince—
> I sang firm—even—Chants—
> I helped his Film—with Hymn—
>
> And when the Dews drew off
> That held his Forehead stiff—
> I met him—
> Balm to Balm—
>
> I told him Best—must pass
> Through this low Arch of Flesh—
> No Casque so brave
> It spurn the Grave—
>
> I told him Worlds I knew
> Where Emperors grew—

> Who recollected us
> If we were true—
>
> And so with Thews of Hymn—
> And Sinew from within—
> And ways I knew not that I knew—till then—
> I lifted Him— (616)[36]

She entices her lover-adversary into death so that she may achieve dominance; she becomes, through her reassuring her prince, a beguiling murderess at last able to assert her own supremacy. This mortal adversary is a combatant, a wrestler, an active lover. And Dickinson's perception of this potentially lethal masculine force is the reflection of Keats's muse, goddess, *femme*. As we have already seen, Keats also views with deep ambivalence the mythic woman who possesses the origins of his poetic afflatus. Dickinson's relation to her other is similarly marked by her fear of his dangerous presence, the possibility of imminent withdrawal. His secrets plague her; his silences threaten to destroy her own voice. The essential distinction between Keats's muse and Dickinson's is that for her the other is father, poet, lover, and Christ. His existence is coextensive with Dickinson's own; she cannot, like Keats, separate female lover from precursor poet.

Keats copes with the pressures of his precursors by insisting upon a sense of progress, a "grand march of intellect" or filial relationship that leads from poetic father to son.[37] He maintains a sense of historicity by placing his precursors firmly yet prophetically in the past. As Walter Jackson Bate remarks, Keats shares in the "immortal freemasonry" of the great in any age; this sense of comraderie and familial descent eases the burden of influence upon him.[38] Certainly Keats

---

[36] An orthodox or canonical reading of this poem would maintain that the "I" acquired new *consolatory* powers in the face of "his" death.

[37] Keats, *Letters*, letter no. 80, I, 282, 3 May 1818, to Reynolds.

[38] See Walter Jackson Bate, *The Burden of the Past and the English Poet* (Cambridge: The Belknap Press of Harvard University Press, 1970), pp. 102 and 129.

The Poet's Romance

suffers in his awareness of Milton's and Wordsworth's achieved genius, but he struggles as a son with his father—one who has inherited the powers he needs to win his individuating freedom.[39] But for Dickinson the precursor becomes a supervening presence. Because her precursor is lover and father, her dependence upon such a doubly potent image—what I earlier called a "composite precursor"—increases her precarious position. Consequently her poems reveal an ongoing attempt to dismiss as she simultaneously absorbs this other. And her sense of progress or development depends upon momentary success; time is defined by crises as liminal moments assume an overwhelming importance, for they define what comes before and after—they are crucial pauses for precaution. The Keatsian faith in the progress of poetry is no longer firm because defeat follows upon victory in cyclical confrontation. Such a conflict must remain unresolved, for the problem Dickinson faces is how to maintain a dialogue with this projected other—composite precursor and internal adversary—while at the same time protecting herself from him lest she be overwhelmed. The precariousness of her position, the necessity simultaneously to woo and to reject, denies her Keats's sense of continuity, his participation in a patriarchal lineage against which she must struggle to assert her poetic authority. Yvor Winters suggests the relation between Dickinson's "problem," as he calls it, and the "solution" of her poems: "It is possible to solve any problem of insoluble experience by retreating a step and defining the boundary at which comprehension ceases, and by then making the necessary moral adjustments to that boundary; this in itself is an experience both final and serious, and it is the experience on which our author's finest work is based."[40] One strategy for establishing new boundaries is to

---

[39] For a further consideration of Keats's relation to his precursors, see Harold Bloom, "Keats and the Embarrassments of Poetic Tradition," (*From Sensibility to Romanticism*, eds. Frederick Hilles and Harold Bloom [London: Oxford University Press, 1965]), 513-526.

[40] Yvor Winters, "Emily Dickinson and the Limits of Judgment," *In Defense of Reason* (Denver: Alan Swallow, 1943), p. 290.

The Poet's Romance

call upon the power to forget. Describing the construction of an independent edifice of the soul, Dickinson writes:

> The Props assist the House
> Until the House is built
> And then the Props withdraw
> And adequate, erect,
> The House support itself
> And cease to recollect
> The Augur and the Carpenter—
> Just such a retrospect
> Hath the perfected Life—
> A past of Plank and Nail
> And slowness—then the Scaffolds drop
> Affirming it a Soul. (1142)

The necessity of ceasing to recollect is a precondition for the existence of the independent structure. Without this forgetting, the presence of the carpenter would haunt the perfected life. A neutral, un-self-conscious house is a numbing metaphor for the poet and her muse. By describing the process of "making a life" in terms of carpenter and wood, Dickinson momentarily defines a conscious boundary to protect her from a threatening self-consciousness. She finds safety in the asexual, mechanical language of craft.

Dickinson also forms a salutary, protective boundary in her garden; the domesticated, magnified landscape of bird, bee, and flower allows her to enact the drama of sexuality freed from overpowering self-consciousness. She chooses this pastoral yet neighboring sphere as her privileged ground, a place where visitation, coupling, and impregnation lose their companions, anxiety and fear. Privilege quickly wanes, however, when Dickinson's own shadow appears on the land.[41] But as long as she preserves the separation of self and

---

[41] Of her relation to her garden, Winters writes: "Occasionally, instead of endeavoring to treat the small subject in terms appropriate to it, she endeavors to treat it in terms appropriate to her own temperament, and we

garden, she has found her plot of sacred ground. Absence of awareness characterizes this landscape; apprehension and remorse disappear when thought is banished. Dickinson's vision of bee and flower echoes Keats's vision of a sexual drama freed from overwhelming anxiety. Openness and peace mark these poets' conceptions of an ideal love that escapes their own divided, threatened perception of human sexuality. The ability to share the pleasures of bee and flower, the freedom to identify with both sides of the couple offer a reassuring possibility:

". . . we should rather be the flower than the Bee—for it is a false notion that more is gained by receiving than giving—no the receiver and the giver are equal in their benefits—The f[l]ower I doubt not receives a fair guerdon from the Bee—its leaves blush deeper in the next spring—and who shall say between Man and Woman which is the most delighted? . . . but let us open our leaves like a flower and be passive and receptive—budding patiently under the eye of Apollo . . . the Morning said I was right—"[42]

Keats assumes the guise of flower to experience the essentially feminine delight of receptivity—the flower that buds under the generative eye of Apollo, masculine force of sun and another avatar of Keats as poet-god. The rising light, the power of the sun as it moves toward its zenith, is proof that his imagination is "right." Dickinson invokes bird, bee, and flower but finds it difficult to maintain the requisite distance between self and nature to preserve the un-self-conscious sanctity of her chosen images. Only rarely can she accept Keats's luxuriant, privileged conception. Instead, she concentrates on the intricacy of the flower and the hazards of natural process. She undermines the pastoral vision by combining a whimsical anthropomorphism, a projection of her own fears, with an acknowledged awareness of the threat

---

have what appears a deliberate excursion into obscurity, the subject being inadequate to the rhetoric, . . ." (pp. 286 ff.) Winters' comments miss, I think, the intention behind Dickinson's interjection of self into language.

[42] Keats, *Letters*, letter no. 62, I, 232, 19 February 1818, to Reynolds.

The Poet's Romance

inherent in life itself. "Bloom" is not to be taken for granted; rather, the growth of the flower is more a defensive management of threatening forces than it is an assured process:

> . . . .
> To pack the Bud—oppose the Worm—
> Obtain it's right of Dew—
> Adjust the Heat—elude the Wind—
> Escape the prowling Bee
>
> Great Nature not to disappoint
> Awaiting Her that Day—
> To be a Flower, is profound
> Responsibility— (1058)

Here Dickinson emphasizes the difficulty of process. Nothing can be assumed, for the destructive possibilities of nature lie always close at hand. The end cannot be assured until it is achieved. When Dickinson identifies bee and flower with lover and beloved, she emphasizes the threat the bee offers the flower; the blossom must adopt the coy excuses of a young lady to control the bee's repeated advances. If the bee approaches the flower's "door" too often, the flower must learn the language of decorous rejection:

> . . . .
> But teach the Footman from Vevay—
> Mistress is 'not at home'—to say—
> To people—any more! (206)

The charade of society is grafted upon organic process. Fear of violation adds to the customary anxiety that the lover will "lose the respect" of the flower once she has succumbed to his demands:

> Did the Harebell loose her girdle
> To the lover Bee
> Would the Bee the Harebell *hallow*
> Much as formerly?

The Poet's Romance

> Did the 'Paradise'—persuaded—
> Yield her moat of pearl—
> Would the Eden *be* an Eden,
> Or the Earl—an *Earl*? (213)

By subverting the common wisdom that the Harebell will lose the bee's respect once she has yielded to him, Dickinson conjectures that the Earl himself and the sacred garden will suffer by the Harebell's surrender. Authority vanishes from bee, flower, and garden once the inevitable compromise is made. This coy intrusion of society's conventions upon the natural union of bee and flower develops into an abiding mode in Dickinson's nature poems—the garden becomes a neutral landscape which may provide freedom from personal anxiety or, hiding behind a mock insouciance, an occasion to allegorize fear.

Moreover, Keats and Dickinson witness the threat within nature itself. Recall, for example, the troubling awareness that results from the poet's looking too deeply into the sea which Keats recounts in his "epistle to Reynolds." Gazing into the ocean, he sees a proto-Darwinian scene enacting the survival of the fittest, a drama that embodies nature's cold disregard for the pains of destruction and death. Tormented by this harsh night vision, he recollects the source of his distress:

> . . . I saw
> Too far into the sea, where every maw
> The greater on the less feeds evermore.—
> But I saw too distinct into the core
> Of an eternal fierce destruction, . . .
> The Shark at savage prey,—the Hawk at pounce,—
> The gentle Robin, like a Pard or Ounce,
> Ravening a worm, . . .[43]

Keats cannot tolerate this vision and fights against its potential ability to destroy his search for a nature at once benefi-

---

[43] Keats, *Poems*, "To J. H. Reynolds Esq.," 11. 93-105.

cent and humane. But he cannot turn to this disturbing and brutally clear acknowledgment of facts for solace. Instead, he creates that alternative nature we have already recognized—a garden of the brain. And it is within this "foliage of the mind" that Keats seeks to woo his beloved.[44] His garden, the realm of "Flora and old Pan," is shaped by permanence, for neither change nor the awareness of process disturbs this imaginative realm. Keats's envy of nature attests to his wish to be freed from the pressures of memory and the anxiety of anticipation. This tension between a craving for permanence and the necessity of change persists and leads to the final resolution Keats achieves in the Odes. This resolution of the desire for stasis and the inevitability of change defines, as Harold Bloom suggests, the poet's new-won freedom from his own poetic tradition:

"What Keats so greatly gives to the Romantic tradition in the *Nightingale* ode is what no poet before him had the capability of giving—the sense of the human making choice of a human self, aware of its deathly nature, and yet having the will to celebrate the imaginative richness of mortality. The *Ode to a Nightingale* is the first poem to know and declare, wholeheartedly, that death is the mother of beauty. The *Ode to Psyche* still glanced, with high good humor, at the haunted rituals of the already written poems of heaven; the *Ode to a Nightingale* turns, almost casually, to the unwritten great poem of earth. There is nothing casual about the poem's tone, but there is a wonderful lack of self-consciousness at the poem's freedom from the past, in the poem's knowing that death, our death, is absolute and without memorial."[45]

Keats's "Ode To Autumn" is the consummate poem of this naturalistic acceptance accompanied by an underlying sense of resignation. Keats, as Bloom states, "perfects an image in which stasis and process are reconciled," and autumn becomes the most human of seasons.[46] Dickinson confronts the

[44] Dickinson, Poem 1634.

[45] Harold Bloom, "Keats and the Embarrassments of Poetic Tradition," *From Sensibility to Romanticism*, p. 520.

[46] *Ibid.*, p. 525.

The Poet's Romance

inexplicable facts of nature, but the conflict she perceives remains unresolved. Indeed, Keats's acceptance, his extraordinary "post-Romantic" vision, forms one side of a continuing dialectic with Dickinson's own defiance.

INITIALLY, Dickinson posits, as had the early Keats, an alternative poetic landscape that offers relief from the pain of this world:

> There is another sky,
> Ever serene and fair,
> And there is another sunshine,
> Though it be darkness there;
> Never mind faded forests, Austin,
> Never mind silent fields—
> *Here* is a little forest,
> Whose leaf is ever green;
> Here is a brighter garden,
> Where not a frost has been;
> In its unfading flowers
> I hear the bright bee hum;
> Prithee, my brother,
> Into *my* garden come! (2)

She creates her "garden in the brain" as Keats his "garden of the mind"; he opens his self-created garden to love and she to her beloved brother. Dickinson retains and insists upon the preeminence of her imaginative landscape, however, for the power of the mind is the requisite force needed to secure her vision. Although Keats makes his peace with nature, she preserves the separation of self and world necessary to her solipsistic defense. With his characteristic insight, Albert Gelpi remarks that although "she might say that she lived in an Eden of unfading seasons and perpetual noon, . . . such a world existed only in her saying it—that is, only in the transcendent ordering of art."[47] From her earliest poems,

---
[47] Gelpi, *Emily Dickinson*, p. 88.

The Poet's Romance

Dickinson asserts the independent sanctity of the imagination. The chief difference between her sphere and nature's is the poet's ability to control process, to render stasis at will.

> There is a Zone whose even Years
> No Solstice interrupt—
> Whose Sun constructs perpetual Noon
> Whose perfect Seasons wait—
>
> Whose Summer set in Summer, till
> The Centuries of June
> And Centuries of August cease
> And Consciousness—is Noon. (1056)

She halts all cyclic process; the seasons do not change, they "wait." Defying expectation, summer will not slip into autumn but lapses into a further summer. The solstice, or turning point, has been replaced by the perpetual noon of imagination. Deflected from its prescribed course, the sun loses power as consciousness usurps its life-giving force—a sovereign Apollo overthrows the laws of natural process. In an earlier poem, Dickinson assesses her priorities and firmly establishes her own poetic primacy:

> I reckon—when I count at all—
> First—Poets—Then the Sun—
> Then Summer—Then the Heaven of God—
> And then—the List is done—
>
> But, looking back—the First so seems
> To Comprehend the Whole—
> The Others look a needless Show—
> So I write—Poets—All—
>
> Their Summer—lasts a Solid Year—
> They can afford a Sun
> The East—would deem extravagant—
> And if the Further Heaven—

The Poet's Romance

> Be Beautiful as they prepare
> For those who worship Them—
> It is too difficult a Grace—
> To justify the Dream— (569)[48]

She reviews her ordering of poet, sun, summer, and heaven to assert that the first subsumes the realm of nature and the promise of heaven. The poet's power depends upon an ability to vanquish process: "Their Summer—lasts a Solid Year—"; only imagination can create a sun which makes faint the fiery star that renders all others invisible. As nature pales beside the power of the poet, so the possibility of another place, a further heaven, proves "too difficult a Grace— / To justify the Dream—". By coupling difficulty and grace, Dickinson alters the received theological concept of a grace freely bestowed by God; here it becomes, instead, a goal toward which one strives with difficulty. This change allows grace to be susceptible to achievement, thus diminishing God's sovereignty. By coupling the Catholic doctrine of works with the Calvinistic concept of Grace, Dickinson weakens either option. She asserts that Grace, freely given, is hardly worth waiting for, but denies the assurance that deeds will be justly rewarded. The promise of a further heaven is tenuous and keeps receding—a promise too remote to justify the dream.

---

[48] Anderson writes: "This poem throws light on the earlier chapters setting forth her esthetic theory. The poet cannot expand to the divine circumference, but he does not need to for he can create his own. His true center is not even the outside world but his consciousness of it, and this inner world is a fiction made with words. She ranked poets first and chose to be one herself because they can create both heaven and earth, a heaven more attainable and a nature more satisfying than any the real world can offer. In this sense only is the poet 'able as God.' This is why she elected to live in the world of perceptions, where she too could be a maker and achieve immortality in her art" (p. 94).

Whether the "choice" is really so simple or so straightforward as Anderson suggests is open to question, but he aptly emphasizes the probable motives behind Dickinson's need to define and inhabit her own poetic landscape.

The Poet's Romance

In the meantime, Keats and Dickinson use the same form, the figure of the spider, to symbolize a precarious self-sufficiency which both separates and connects them to the natural world. First Keats:

"Now it appears to me that almost any Man may like the Spider spin from his own inwards his own airy Citadel—the points of leaves and twigs on which the Spider begins her work are few and she fills the Air with a beautiful circuiting: man should be content with as few points to tip with the fine Webb of his Soul and weave a tapestry empyrean—full of Symbols for his spiritual eye, of softness for his spiritual touch, of space for his wandering of distinctness for his Luxury—"[49]

Although the spider serves as an example of how little one need rely upon external nature for support, Keats still maintains that a few points, the outline of bare twigs, are needed to form the limits of man's "beautiful circuiting." Nature is present, if barely so; the imagination begins in the landscape, but through its inner weaving opens up infinite possibilities. Dickinson's spider displays its complete self-sufficiency as well as the lack of appreciation that follows his art. Informed by the "white arc" of the self alone, he creates in darkness:

> A Spider sewed at Night
> Without a Light
> Upon an Arc of White.
>
> If Ruff it was of Dame
> Or Shroud of Gnome
> Himself himself inform.
>
> Of Immortality
> His Strategy
> Was Physiognomy. (1138)

This spider at once gives the web both its function and its importance; completely dependent upon its maker for its

---

[49] Keats, *Letters*, letter no. 62, I, 231-232, 19 February 1818, to J. H. Reynolds.

The Poet's Romance

physical shape, the web becomes a mirror of the artist's features. The performing spider makes his claim for immortality by creating an external vision of himself, a conjectural portrait of the weaver in the web.[50] Deprived of recognition and a receptive audience, Dickinson joins hands with the spider. Housewives, caretakers of a Christian nation, thoughtlessly destroy the spider's work, a warning to any poet who might be tempted to offer her poems to a callous, conforming public.

> The Spider as an Artist
> Has never been employed—
> Though his surpassing Merit
> Is freely certified
>
> By every Broom and Bridget
> Throughout a Christian Land—
> Neglected Son of Genius
> I take thee by the Hand— (1275)

Unnoticed, the spider makes his presence felt; his webs inform the corners of unwelcoming rooms. Unappreciated and therefore totally independent, the spider is Dickinson's image of the working poet—one who despite the most persistent efforts of the caretakers of convention keeps forming poems out of the solitary self. In such isolation, the poet is free to create a completely autonomous place, a region inhabited solely by the self and what the self needs to feed upon.

Dickinson redefines the terms of her world to create a stasis in which the poet strives to diminish anxiety by slowing time, freezing the process on the brink of fulfillment. Like the figure on Keats's Grecian Urn, she remains a "still unravish'd bride of quietness."[51] But Keats expresses in this

---

[50] See Anderson, p. 126.

[51] Discussing this desire, Gelpi (*Emily Dickinson*) suggests that such a perception would allow Dickinson to create a sphere in which "one can have the passion without the exhaustion, the commitment without the consum-

ode and elsewhere the frigidity of an art that submits to a seductive permanence which offers the comfort of an eternal beauty but also a cold silence that can answer no questions, a world where life's procession leads to no final goal. Of the march of the "mysterious priest and the sacrificial heifer" on the Grecian Urn, Helen Vendler writes that it is a "procession with no *terminus a quo,* no *terminus ad quem,* only the endless intent to sacrifice, itself incapable of execution, since that too is a goal. . . ."[52] In order to create such stillness, there must be a crucial "sacrifice of life to art."[53] Keats's Ode acknowledges the loss as it reveals the beauty of the silent urn. But Dickinson is willing to move further into this perfect realm than Keats, with his human reservations, is willing to go. Dressed in white—raiment of virginity and God's chosen—she proclaims herself the "wife without the sign" and so assumes the persona of Keats's projection of aesthetic stasis. In the poems, this Dickinsonian image is both the maiden on the urn and the urn itself, conveyor of art as well as the drawing upon it.[54] She desires the "wild ecstasy" of immortality and the power to bear witness to that ecstasy in a world that will not admit change. Once expectation is consummated and longing achieved, all is lost.

> Dominion lasts until obtained—
> Possession just as long—
> But these—endowing as they flit
> Eternally belong.
>
> How everlasting are the Lips
> Known only to the Dew—
> These are the Brides of permanence
> Supplanting me and you (1257)

---

mation" (p. 118). As Keats wishes to escape the "fever and the fret" of life, so Dickinson desires to avoid the necessary accompanying results of her emotions.

[52] Helen Vendler, "The Experiential Beginnings of Keats's Odes," *Studies in Romanticism,* II, 3 (Summer, 1973), p. 601.

[53] *Ibid.*   [54] Dickinson, Poem 1072.

The Poet's Romance

The lesson is clear: anticipation surpasses fulfillment and so should be preserved. Desire alone assures permanence. Late in life, Dickinson writes to her friend and beloved suitor, Judge Otis Lord: "Don't you know you are happiest while I withhold and not confer—don't you know that 'No' is the wildest word we consign to Language?"[55] Dickinson's emphasis on wildness, on an intensity surpassing satiety, finds a response in Keats's words. For him, too, the ultimate force is not undifferentiated bliss or all-consuming evil; the power of experience depends upon energy: "the excellence of every Art is its intensity, capable of making all disagreeables evaporate, from their being in close relationship with Beauty & Truth—Examine King Lear & you will find this examplified throughout; . . ."[56]

Keats's allusion to *Lear* clarifies his assertion; he is not concerned with pure states of luxuriance or the commonplace dichotomy of pleasure and pain. Furthermore, this intensity predates any single emotion and is the foundation of Keats's own stance. The energy behind the Keatsian vision of fullness informs his view of grief lying in the lap of pleasure, a fusion of a potentially disruptive coupling. The basis for this perception is, of course, Keats's continued awareness of the presence of death. In such a world, what value can the poet assign to any single moment? "I scarcely remember counting upon any Happiness—I look not for it if it be not in the present hour—nothing startles me beyond the Moment. The setting sun will always set me to rights—or if a Sparrow come before my Window I take part in its existence and pick about the Gravel."[57]

In one poem, Dickinson expresses her disapproval of such an escape into the present, a willingness to enter into the life of the sparrow. She retorts:

---

[55] Dickinson, letter no. 562, II, 617, about 1878, to Otis P. Lord.
[56] Keats, *Letters*, letter no. 45, I, 192, 21, 27(?) December 1817, to George and Tom Keats.
[57] Keats, *Letters*, letter no. 43, I, 186, 22 November 1817, to Benjamin Bailey.

The Poet's Romance

> How much the present moment means
> To those who've nothing more—
> The Fop—the Carp—the Atheist—
> Stake an entire store
> Upon a Moment's shallow Rim
> While their commuted Feet
> The Torrents of Eternity
> Do all but inundate— (1380)

The vehemence of this response conveys her abhorrence of the notion that she enjoy or even seek solace in the moment for its own sake. This may strike us as rather odd in a poet who so often makes a single moment the occasion for her poems. But a crucial distinction exists between those she criticizes and her own approach to experience, for Dickinson charges such moments with an intensity whose source lies in her desire to wrest from the experience a knowledge that evades more conventional methods of inquiry. To say the moment is enough in itself would border on heresy, because it is not the solace of forgetfulness but just its opposite that Dickinson hopes to win. A poetics based on invocation cannot be synonymous, though it may at first resemble, one that advocates an unburdened giving of the self to experience.

ELSEWHERE Dickinson appears directly to challenge Keats's consolatory perspective in a poem that may be interpreted as a refutation of the benignity at the heart of his poetic vision. "On the Grasshopper and the Cricket," which Keats composed in the depths of winter, celebrates the cycle of renewal, the recurrence of song that passes from the birds of summer to the grasshopper and, during the "long winter evening," to the cricket in the hearth. On this cold winter night, the cricket sings from the source of warmth; to the poet "in drowsiness half lost," the insect becomes the grasshopper singing "among some grassy hills." The warmth of the stove, projected by the increasingly intense singing of the cricket, leads the drowsy poet back into summer. The poem opens by asserting that "The Poetry of earth is never dead," a statement which, in its boldness and finality, prophesies the opening lines of *Endymion*.[58] "On the Grasshopper and the Cricket" conveys reassurance; the faint birds "hide in cooling trees," the grasshopper takes "the lead / In summer luxury," the only weariness results from "fun." Dickinson echoes this poem but transposes the voice of the cricket into a somber sound:[59]

> Further in Summer than the Birds
> Pathetic from the Grass
> A minor Nation celebrates
> It's unobtrusive Mass.
>
> No Ordinance be seen
> So gradual the Grace
> A pensive Custom it becomes
> Enlarging Loneliness.
>
> Antiquest felt at Noon
> When August burning low
> Arise this spectral Canticle
> Repose to typify
>
> Remit as yet no Grace
> No Furrow on the Glow
> Yet a Druidic Difference
> Enhances Nature now (1068)

[58] The lines to which I refer are, of course:
> A thing of beauty is a joy for ever:
> Its loveliness increases; it will never
> Pass into nothingness; but still will keep
> A bower quiet for us, and a sleep
> Full of sweet dreams, and health, and quiet breathing.

The opening of *Endymion* is a statement of Keats's most beneficent vision of the possibilities of art. The sonnet "On the Grasshopper and Cricket" reflects his sense of the restorative powers of nature.

[59] Winters (*In Defense of Reason*) comments on Dickinson's poem: ". . . the subject is the plight of man, the willing and freely moving entity, in a universe in which he is by virtue of his essential qualities a foreigner. The intense nostalgia of the poem is the nostalgia of man for the mode of being which he perceives imperfectly and in which he cannot share" (p. 292).

Sending this poem along with another to Thomas Niles, the Boston publisher, Dickinson comments, "I bring you a chill Gift—My Cricket—and the Snow—."[60] Her "chill Gift" takes as its subject the same song of the cricket that had cheered Keats; but, listening in late summer, she hears the sounds of loss, the death of her beloved season. Once birds have ceased singing, the "pathetic crickets," a "minor"—melancholy, insignificant—nation, celebrate their own mass over the dying day. Keats had stressed the continuity of bird and cricket; Dickinson emphasizes the fall from the free, singing birds to the lowly inhabitants of the grass. The poem describes the mass, which should be magisterial, as pathetic and meager, thus deepening the pensive quality of the crickets' cries. As the song gradually mounts, it fills the landscape with loneliness. Keats's cricket sang with increasing intensity of a reassuring companionship; Dickinson's expresses loss. This "spectral Cantical" imperceptibly transforms the landscape as the sense of ancient, buried time whelms the late summer day. The crickets at noon prophesy the advent of evening; their song promises a departure which alters the land: "Yet a Druidic Difference / Enhances Nature now." From the cold winter night, Keats's cricket offered the hope of a renewed summer; each season gives way to the next in a changing but benign cycle. Dickinson's cricket speaks of cycles, too. But in her poem loss predominates—the pain of departure which simultaneously recalls mortality and the particular vision such awareness conveys.

Rather than accepting the cyclical movement of the seasons, Dickinson responds to change in terms that suggest her desire for control, not only of herself but of time as well. Elsewhere (in Poem 1540) Dickinson characterizes the decline of summer as a betrayal. Not only the poet but nature itself mourns the end of a season. Summer passes "as imperceptibly as grief," and what alone keeps us from feeling this

---

[60] Dickinson, letter no. 813, III, 768, mid-March 1883, to Thomas Niles. The other poem she enclosed was "It sifts from Leaden Sieves." (Poem 311.)

departure as a betrayal is its silent and slow decline.[61] Having evaded all attempts to hold her, the summer departs, enabling her to escape the cycles of nature to enter the realm of the "Beautiful." The season moves into the abstract sphere of thought sanctified by memory, the saving imagination, and the retrospective vision of Beauty. The pain of summer's passing provokes Dickinson to assume a determining power over the past as well as the future, so she extends the province of her artistic control by shaping memory according to desire. To T. W. Higginson, her friend and preceptor, she writes: "To hope with the Imagination is inevitable, but to remember—with it is the most consecrated ecstasy of the Will—"[62] The transforming power of the imagination must not be confused with a fatal self-deception rooted in the need to distort reality to make it more palatable. Dickinson insists upon facing the full burden of reality, the contradictory condition of experience. Negative capability is as necessary for her as it is for Keats. And it is that necessity which impels us to read her in the context he has created. For both, negative capability combines an inclusive receptivity, a refusal to take sides, and the willingness to lose one's individuality in unmediated experience. Both are aware of the difficulties of such a commitment, and Dickinson faces the absolute necessity of remaining immune to the temptation of false, comforting delusions. Wonder, for Dickinson, is "a beautiful but bleak condition"—the essence of life: "He has not lived who has not felt." Yet when this wonder matures into suspense, the Adult vision turns dark:

> . . . .
> Suspense—is his maturer Sister—
> Whether Adult Delight is Pain
> Or of itself a new misgiving—
> This is the Gnat that mangles men— (1331)

---

[61] See Dickinson, Poem 1540.
[62] Dickinson, letter no. 574, II, 627, early November 1878, to T. W. Higginson.

Dickinson not only embraces "wonder," but, recognizing the character of her intellect, she asserts her own need to pursue a constantly questioning existence. To her sister-in-law Sue, she writes, "In a Life that stopped guessing, you and I should not feel at home."[63] Dickinson conveys the essential spirit of Keatsian negative capability but with a crucial difference. First Keats's definition: "that is when man is capable of being in uncertainties, Mysteries, doubts, without any irritable reaching after fact & reason—."[64] This most assuredly is to live in the realm of "not precisely Knowing / And not precisely Knowing not." But Dickinson asks "whether Adult Delight is Pain," thereby acknowledging the proximate relation of joy and grief, for she is unsure whether by definition adult delight is pain, or whether her own mistrust of happiness creates her uneasiness. This comingling of delight and pain becomes a descriptive technique in Keats's and Dickinson's poems, where the symbiosis of opposition informs their mutual perception of how one learns to live.[65]

Even when the tawdry realities of money impinge upon his ambition, Keats is able to incorporate such difficulties

---

[63] Dickinson, letter no. 586, II, 632, about 1878, to Susan Gilbert Dickinson.

[64] Keats, *Letters*, letter no. 45, I, 193, 27(?) December 1817, to George and Tom Keats.

[65] Negative Capability has darker implications as well. Loss of self, a diminishing identity, can threaten the poet as he seeks to enter into the experience before him. Discussing Dickinson's work, John Cody, in *After Great Pain: The Inner Life of Emily Dickinson* (Cambridge: Harvard University Press, 1971), writes: "The common denominator in all these 'sea poems,' however, regardless of the pleasurability of the feeling, is the poet's experience of a diffusion of herself—of the blurring of her own boundaries until she becomes lost in the infinite or expands into infinity herself" (p. 304).

Keats experiences a similar diminution of the sense of self: ". . . the poet has none; no identity—he is certainly the most unpoetical of all God's Creatures. If then he has no self, and if I am a Poet, where is the Wonder that I should say I would write [right] no more? . . When I am in a room with People if I ever am free from speculating on creations of my own brain, then not myself goes home to myself: but the identity of every one in the room begins to press upon me that, I am in a very little time anhilated—" (*Letters*, letter no. 118, I, 387, 27 October 1818, to Richard Woodhouse).

The Poet's Romance

into his vision of a better life. Discussing these difficulties with his friend Benjamin Haydon, Keats remarks of "that bill-pestilence": "However I must think that difficulties nerve the Spirit of a Man—they make our Prime Objects a Refuge as well as a Passion."[66] Besides enhancing our final goals, suffering becomes an essential condition to achieve a more humane wisdom, the beginning of mature poetic vision: "for axioms in philosophy are not axioms until they are proved upon our pulses: We read fine—things but never feel them to thee full until we have gone the same steps as the Author. . . ."[67] What makes us better readers makes us better writers. Keats asserts that only through excess do we learn how much is enough, and that suffering is essential for a deeply felt sympathy: "Until we are sick, we understand not;—in fine, as Byron says, 'Knowledge is Sorrow'; and I go on to say that 'Sorrow is Wisdom'—and further for aught we can know for certainty!"[68] This pulse of feeling spurred by pain is Dickinson's dominant mode of definition. Her "life of sensations" implies an anguish that leads to an understanding of the reverse state of happiness, a typically antithetical process.

> To learn the Transport by the Pain—
> As Blind Men learn the sun!
> To die of thirst—suspecting
> That Brooks in Meadows run!
>
> To stay the homesick—homesick feet
> Upon a foreign shore—
> Haunted by native lands, the while—
> And blue—beloved air!
>
> This is the Sovreign Anguish!
> This—the signal wo!
> These are the patient 'Laureates'
> Whose voices—trained—below—

[66] Keats, *Letters*, letter no. 26, I, 141, 10 May 1817, to B. R. Haydon.
[67] Keats, *Letters*, letter no. 80, I, 279, 3 May 1818, to J. H. Reynolds.
[68] *Ibid.*, p. 279.

The Poet's Romance

> Ascend in ceaseless Carol—
> Inaudible, indeed,
> To us—the duller scholars
> Of the Mysterious Bard! (167)

Dickinson proclaims that anguish is fundamental to the sublime, patient "laureates"—the poets of the dead. Their sanctified voices pass, inaudible, beyond the poets of earth, the "duller scholars / Of the Mysterious Bard." But both the poets of the living and their masters in death are students of the chief ante-poet, God. Those poets who have passed through death speak directly to the mysterious Bard; their lingering compatriots can attend only to what they know—the pain of their earthly existence. And those who wish to win the "Sovereign Anguish" must learn from suffering the lessons of the supreme poets who have toiled before them.

Behind these antithetical descriptions of how we learn lies the common premise that intimate experience of life will teach us what we need to know. Keats writes, "I will call the *world* a School . . . the Heart . . . it is the Minds Bible, it is the Minds experience, it is the teat from which the Mind or intelligence sucks its identity—".[69] But Dickinson transforms the world into another kind of school where lessons remain a mystery; therefore the meaning of anguish can be revealed only after she has stopped wondering what it might be.

> I shall know why—when Time is over—
> And I have ceased to wonder why—
> Christ will explain each separate anguish
> In the fair schoolroom of the sky—
>
> He will tell me what 'Peter' promised—
> And I—for wonder at his woe—
> I shall forget the drop of Anguish
> That scalds me now—that scalds me now! (193)

---

[69] Keats, *Letters*, letter no. 159, II, 102-103, 21 April 1819, to the George Keatses.

The Poet's Romance

The final cry, a Keatsian repetition, signals her despair. Explanations lie beyond the province of the possible; they come too late to assuage her pain. Keats also knows that life can scald as well as nourish, that delectable nectar may lie embedded in danger: "Even bees, the little almsmen of spring-bowers, / Know there is richest juice in poison-flowers."[70] But the milk of the mother, the nectar of the blossom, is not to be trusted, for the moment of fulfillment, the climax of pleasure, may suddenly prove lethal: ". . . and aching Pleasure nigh, / Turning to Poison while the bee-mouth sips: . . ."[71] The threat of poison is the converse to the danger of starvation: "There never liv'd a mortal man, who bent / His appetite beyond his natural sphere, / But starv'd and died."[72] Here Keats finds oral deprivation an adequate sentence for the sin of intellectual pride, a judgment that would condemn the terms of Dickinson's search beyond the limits of the known and familiar earth.[73]

IN KEATS's early "Ode to Apollo," it is the proto-bard who usurps the female role and gives birth to his poem:[74]

> But when *Thou* joinest with the Nine,
> And all the powers of song combine,
>   We listen here on earth:
> The dying tones that fill the air,
> And charm the ear of evening fair,
> From thee, great God of Bards, receive
>   their heavenly birth.[75]

---

[70] Keats, "Isabella; Or, the Pot of Basil," XIII, 11. 7-8.

[71] Keats, "Ode on Melancholy," III, 11. 3-4.

[72] Keats, *Endymion*, IV, 11. 646-48.

[73] In Poem 782 Dickinson again uses the image of the poisoned honey and the hungry bee.

[74] The basis of Keats's images of birth, breast, and mother may, as Aileen Ward suggests, lie in his devotion to his own erratic and ailing mother. Ward cites a remark Keats "guardedly made to a 'close friend' that his greatest misfortune" since childhood was that "he had no mother." Aileen Ward, *John Keats: The Making of a Poet* (New York: The Viking Press, 1963), p. 10.

[75] Keats, "Ode to Apollo," 11. 42-47.

The Poet's Romance

The poet here is both father and son, source of nutritive strength as well as of inspiration. Dickinson also associates poetic activity with the oral image of sucking, and, negatively, with maternal deprivation, and the loss of affection. Speaking of her own parent, she comments to Higginson: "I never had a mother. I suppose a mother is one to whom you hurry when you are troubled."[76] Her denial of ever having a mother is disquietingly close to Keats's guarded admission that "he had no mother." But Dickinson's sense of deprivation extends beyond Keats's as she contends that she has always felt such a loss.[77] "I had been hungry, all the Years—" Dickinson asserts. Yet when her Noon finally comes, her "first supper," she has learned to dine without food. Indeed, as Dickinson writes later in the same poem, "The Plenty hurt me—'twas so new—"; the prospect of satiety itself causes pain. Hunger is Dickinson's strategy for overcoming her earlier exclusion from the communion table, an exclusion from those who freely dine together in "fellowship." Thus, Dickinson cannot relinquish her acknowledged hunger because it has become a way of satisfying the starvation such exclusion implies:

> Nor was I hungry—so I found
> That Hunger—was a way
> Of Persons outside Windows—
> The Entering—takes away— (579)

Present and plentiful food overwhelms her; instead, she chooses the absence which makes the present "mean." Ful-

[76] Dickinson, letter no. 342b, II, 475, 1870, T W. Higginson to his wife after visiting with Dickinson.

[77] Of this sense of loss, Gelpi writes, "almost the first act of the mind was an awareness of isolation" (p. 69). Discussing the strength of deprivation, Gelpi wonders: "How could loss be power beyond possession? Because loss made us desire, made us project an object for our desire, made us strain urgently toward it. What we lacked we wanted, and if we lacked all, we wanted all. Fulfillment was static, like eternity; but desire was a process, and was therefore the prerequisite and condition of human life" (p. 71.) See Poem 579 from which the following lines that appear in the text are drawn.

The Poet's Romance

fillment offers confusion and leads to a desire for the earlier and necessary acuity of the starving won at the cost of pain. In "It would have starved a Gnat," hunger turns into a parasite; the leech cannot be coaxed to leave, nor does the host possess the power to escape.[78] A necessary and by now familiar symbiosis results, a condition of mutual dependency based not on the need to survive but on the impossibility of separation. Starvation drains the child's strength as well as her will to live. And a crucial dependency is subverted as need feeds upon the self. Dickinson identifies food with the growth of the poet—words provide his meat, the source of his energy:[79]

> He ate and drank the precious Words—
> His Spirit grew robust—
> He knew no more that he was poor,
> Nor that his frame was Dust—
>
> He danced along the dingy Days
> And this Bequest of Wings
> Was but a Book—What Liberty
> A loosened spirit brings— (1587)

Unable to subsist on the food provided, Dickinson turns within. Thus the strictures of circumstance afford the occasion for a complete reliance upon the self.[80]

---

[78] See Dickinson, Poem 612.

[79] Joseph Lyman had received Dickinson's account of her experience upon returning home after she had been treated in Boston for an eye ailment. Allowed to read once again, she records her homecoming (Richard Sewall, *The Lyman Letters* [Amherst: University of Massachusetts Press, 1965], p. 76): "Going home I flew to the shelves and devoured the luscious passages. I thought I should tear the leaves out as I turned them. Then I settled down to a willingness for all the rest to go but William Shakespear."

[80] Such a reliance upon the self led to a rejection of former need. Dickinson writes:

> Art thou the thing I wanted?
> Begone—my Tooth has grown—
> Supply the minor Palate

The Poet's Romance

Bound by necessity, Dickinson finds requisite internal energy to break through imposed, arbitrary confinement. She struggles for release as from a cocoon that threatens to smother her. And this image of Chrysalis and butterfly recalls Keats's metaphor for his perception of the causes of a temporary setback in his work: "I have of late been moulting: not for fresh feathers & wings: they are gone, and in their stead I hope to have a pair of patient sublunary legs. I have altered, not from a Chrysalis into a butterfly, but the Contrary. having two little loopholes, whence I may look out into the stage of the world: and that world on [my] our coming here I almost forgot."[81]

And Dickinson:

> My Cocoon tightens—Colors teaze—
> I'm feeling for the Air—
> A dim capacity for Wings
> Demeans the Dress I wear—
>
> A power of Butterfly must be—
> The Aptitude to fly
> Meadows of Majesty concedes
> And easy Sweeps of Sky—
>
> So I must baffle at the Hint
> And cipher at the Sign
> And make much blunder, if at last
> I take the clue divine— (1099)

Aptitude to fly signifies the power of the achieved poet; the "eagle of the skies" who soars on extended wings has escaped binding constraints as well as the limitations of grav-

---

> That has not starved so long—
> I tell thee while I waited
> The mystery of Food
> Increased till I abjured it
> And dine without Like God—

A second draft of the poem reveals even stronger language. See Poem 1282.

[81] Keats, *Letters*, letter no. 175, II, 128, 11 July, 1819, to J. H. Reynolds.

The Poet's Romance

ity. Keats also uses the image of flight when he envisions his ideal, the poet unfettered by the bonds of a sessile reality. He calls upon Shakespeare, "Chief Poet," and "ye clouds of Albion" to save him from futile wandering "in a barren dream":[82] "But, when I am consumed in the fire, / Give me new Phoenix wings to fly at my desire."[83] He is unwilling to endure the split of body and soul, the sacrificial psychomachy Dickinson undergoes and which forms her dominant struggle. Threatened by the possibility of internal division, Keats calls to the "God of the Meridian" to reunite his soul, which has "flown," while his body "earthward press'd." The result of this separation causes "a terrible division; [which] leaves a gulph austere / To be fill'd with worldly fear."[84] Flight under such conditions signifies the abandonment of the soul; instead of offering an image of expansive achievement, the eagle turns predator, an abductor of the "young infant child" of the imagination, "And is not this the cause / Of madness?"[85] To control such unbridled escape of the spirit, Keats goes to the God of song, begging that he temper his vision and leave him "more unalarm'd." Once this division is healed, the poet can spread his wings without fear. The eagle is no longer a threat but becomes a symbol of the poet's supreme, unencumbered power. Keats yearns for his fellow poets to soar above blinding constraint, to abandon the branch upon which they sit hooting into the dark, for the freedom of light—"Why should we be owls, when we can be Eagles?" In the early poem "I stood tip-toe," Keats himself is poised for this departure as he prepares to take off toward becoming a poet. He covets the grace of wings,

---

[82] Dickinson also testifies to the overwhelming importance of Shakespeare. She writes to her cousins Louise and Frances Norcross, in 1870, "This little sheet of paper has lain for several years in my Shakespeare, and though it is blotted and antiquated is endeared by it's resting-place." (Jay Leyda, *The Years and Hours of Emily Dickinson*, II [New Haven: Yale University Press, 1960], p. 148) Throughout her letters, there are numerous indications of Dickinson's debt to and admiration of Shakespeare.

[83] Keats, "On Sitting Down To Read King Lear Once Again," 11. 13-14.
[84] Keats, "God of The Meridian," see 11. 1-8.
[85] *Ibid.*, 11. 16-17.

source of strength and balance. He asks in "Sleep and Poetry" what could be "More strange, more beautiful, more smooth, more regal, / Than wings of swans, than doves, than dim-seen eagle."[86] At the poem's close, he describes the bliss of Petrarch and Laura:

> . . . Most happy they!
> For over them was seen a free display
> Of out-spread wings, and from between them shone
> The face of Poesy: . . .[87]

Conversely, in "Hyperion," loss of power and dejection cause Apollo to bemoan his earthbound plight:

> '. . . For me, dark, dark,
> 'And painful vile oblivion seals my eyes:
> 'I strive to search wherefore I am so sad,
> 'Until a melancholy numbs my limbs;
> 'And then upon the grass I sit, and moan,
> 'Like one who once had wings. . . .[88]

Blindness and numbing paralysis overcome the once-soaring god. When Apollo "reads" the history in Mnemosyne's face, he undergoes a painful rebirth; his body verges into metamorphosis:

> During the pain Mnemosyne upheld
> Her arms as one who prophesied.—At length
> Apollo shriek'd;—and lo! from all his limbs
> Celestial. . . .[89]

The poem breaks off as Apollo is about to become the flaming god he once had been. This soaring bird not only is the climactic vision of the poet but also embodies the image of the lover as he strives to win his beloved:

[86] Keats, "Sleep and Poetry," 11. 21-22.
[87] Ibid., 11. 391-394.
[88] Keats, Hyperion, III, 11. 86-91.   [89] Ibid., 11. 133-136.

The Poet's Romance

> How shall I do
> To get anew
> Those moulted feathers, and so mount once more
> Above, above
> The reach of fluttering Love,
> And make him cower lowly while I soar?[90]

His own "winged psyche" seeks a way to overpower the god of love in order to achieve a preeminence which diminishes his rival's diminutive "fluttering."

For Dickinson such flight alone will not suffice. Instead, she must supersede her opponents and mount above her lovers. Flight brings an escape that permits a radical independence, a freedom which insures vital privacy. The young poet is an earthbound "phebe" who nibbles on small "italic seeds," crumbs left by the foreign tongues of other poets.[91] Once she has learned to fly, the poet relinquishes both the need for another and the union of her own body and soul. The prison of circumstances—eternal sustenance and the burden of the body—must be endured only until she makes her escape. Once the poet can soar, Dickinson revels in the division of the body and soul that Keats rejects. Freed from the strictures of mortality, the soul "at Liberty" soars to its freedom. External limitation cannot stay the flight of the inner spirit, no matter what the confines imposed on the physical self. Only the self within has the power to bind or release the desiring soul: "Captivity is Consciousness—/ So's Liberty" (384).

Imprisonment or freedom is an internal condition depending entirely upon one's consciousness. It demands effort, a decisive period of trial, to attain the power of such self-control. The inner body remains inviolate, protected from the mangling hand which destroys its outer form. Imprisonment and the possibility of escape rely upon the outcome of the internal war of self with soul. Responding to the chafing

---

[90] Keats, "To—" ('What can I do to drive away'), 11. 19-24.
[91] See Anderson, pp. 63-64 for the identification of "italic" with foreign.

The Poet's Romance

boundaries of existence, the poet discovers her potential for both flight and song:

> Bind me—I still can sing—
> Banish—my mandolin
> Strikes true within—
>
> Slay—and my Soul shall rise
> Chanting to Paradise—
> Still thine. (1005)

The "I" remains true to the beloved murderer who frees her soul from the constraints of the body. Even without him, she can achieve her metamorphosis into a poet. But this metamorphosis requires time; it is not a miracle spontaneously wrought. Once the freedom to choose becomes fact, she is willingly baptized and rises to a regal status which combines religious sanction with her own individual triumph:

> . . . .
> Baptized, before, without the choice,
> But this time, consciously, of Grace—
> Unto supremest name—
> Called to my Full—The Crescent dropped—
> Existence's whole Arc, filled up,
> With one small Diadem.
>
> My second Rank—too small the first—
> Crowned—Crowing—on my Father's breast—
> A half unconscious Queen—
> But this time—Adequate—Erect,
> With Will to choose, or to reject,
> And I choose, just a Crown— (508)

The crowned rooster crowing on her father's breast is especially evocative. The father prone, his daughter stands upon her defeated progenitor, rejoicing in their relative positions. Having vanquished him in order to attain her confirmed identity, she crows her supremacy—a regal, chosen queen.

The Poet's Romance

Her second baptism, of choice, is more Catholic than her first. In defiance she chooses to wear a symbol anathema to Protestant faith—the crown of Mary and Christ—emblem of Divine sanctity as well as of the conquering poet.[92] Dickinson adopts the accoutrements of royalty (crown, robe, throne) to complete her image which transfers the symbols of secular as well as religious power to the poet.

Dickinson covets the diadem of authority, a desire which parallels Keats's own wish for a laurel wreath signifying poetic supremacy and public recognition.[93] Apollo, god of light and the lyre, wears the laurels that Keats covets; Dickinson values the diadem as a befitting adornment of a female poet of great stature. This diadem is the feminine form of Apollo's laurels; for it is the god of light whom Keats invokes that she too reveres.[94] According to the *Archaeologica*

---

[92] There is an antithetical side to the symbols of crown and wreath for both Dickinson and Keats Dickinson envisions a diadem of daisies which will crown her head after she is buried:

> Here, where the Daisies fit my Head
> 'Tis easiest to lie
> And every Grass that plays outside
> Is sorry, some, for me.
>
> Where I am not afraid to go
> I may confide my Flower—
> Who was not Enemy of Me
> Will gentle be, to Her
>
> Nor separate, Herself and Me
> By Distances become—
> A single Bloom we constitute
> Departed, or at Home— (1037)

Keats acknowledges the wreath that binds him to the earth as well as the laurels that mark his poetic achievement.

[93] For the anecdote of Keats's crowning himself with the laurel, see Bate, *John Keats*, pp. 136-140.

[94] Dickinson associates the light of the sun with the fulfillment of the poet; Keats characterizes his striving toward poetic attainment in terms of light and darkness (Keats, *Letters*, letter no. 159, II, 80, 19 March 1819, to the George Keatses): "I am however young writing at random—straining at particles of light in the midst of a great darkness—. . . ."

Graeca, "the chewing of laurel leaves induces both poetic and erotic frenzy in which the Pythian priestess spoke his oracles in verse."[95] The laurel was also said to have the power to induce dreams. This intoxication of the poet, the "frenzy" of creativity, is what Keats desires when he crowns himself with the symbolic wreath. The image of poetic intoxication fuses with the eucharistic function of the holy wine, which, as Mario D'Avanzo suggests, provides Keats's Apollo with divine knowledge "as if some blithe wine / or bright elixir peerless I had drunk, / And so become immortal. . . ."[96] Keats's poet enjoys the intoxication of inspiration as he partakes in the sanctity of religious offering.[97] However, Dickinson substitutes the wine of the spirit for the more naturalistic grape. She rejects all external intoxicants because no such sacrament can offer what she needs:

>   Exhiliration—is within—
>   There can no Outer Wine
>   So royally intoxicate
>   As that diviner Brand
>
>   The Soul achieves—Herself—
>   To drink—or set away
>   For Visiter—Or Sacrament—
>   'Tis not of Holiday
>
>   To stimulate a Man
>   Who hath the Ample Rhine
>   Within his Closet—Best you can
>   Exhale in offering. (383)

[95] See D'Avanzo, p. 104.
[96] *Ibid.*, p. 110.
[97] See David Perkins, *The Quest for Permanence· The Symbolism of Wordsworth, Shelley, and Keats* (Cambridge: Harvard University Press, 1959), p. 248, for a discussion of the relation of wine to poetry, imagination, and happiness in Keats's writing. For further discussions of Keats's fusing of religious language and the poetic enterprise see Bate, *John Keats*, pp. 136, 148 and Keats, *Letters*, letter no. 41, I, 179, 3 November 1817, to Benjamin Bailey and letter no. 285, II, 323, 16 August 1820, to Percy Bysshe Shelley.

The Poet's Romance

She chooses to provide her own sacrament, rather than accept the stimulation of an inferior, external brand. To her mythic "visitor," she will offer only the wine of the self as a match for his own ample store. Imbued with religious authority and a pagan energy, the poet assumes preeminence for Keats and for Dickinson.

NOT SURPRISINGLY, such an authoritative vision of the poet intensifies the pressure on the self as it struggles to reach the goal of a private divinity. The passivity which tempts Keats and the indolence into which he may sink emerge from the burden placed upon him by his own conception of the poet. Suffering from his vision of what he strives to attain—the soaring stature of the poet-god—Keats reiterates his envy of un-self-conscious trees which possess "the feel of not to feel it."[98] In his lines to Reynolds cited above Keats concludes:

---

[98] The edition of Keats circulating during Dickinson's lifetime printed the line, "To know the pain and feel it." It was corrected in subsequent editions of Keats's poems. Although no copy of Keats's poems belonging to Dickinson has been found, the Dickinson family owned Charles A. Dana's *Household Book of Verse* (N.Y.: D. Appleton & Co., 1860) and Robert Chambers' *Cyclopaedia of English Literature* (London & Edinburgh, 1853), both of which contained several of Keats's poems. The Northampton Library (whose records of borrowers from this period are lost) did have an 1848 edition of Lord Houghton's *Life, Letters and Literary Remains by John Keats* as well as the pirated Galignani edition of *The Poetical Works of Coleridge, Shelley, and Keats, Complete in One Volume* (Paris, 1829, reprinted in America). In his "Letter to a Young Contributor" (*Atlantic Monthly*, April 1862), Thomas Wentworth Higginson admonished young poets to emulate Keats; Dickinson responded in her letter asking that Higginson help her evaluate her own poetry by stating that of the writers she most admired, for poets, she had Keats. The *Atlantic* published two other articles that may have influenced Dickinson's conception of the poet. The first, "Recollections of Keats," by "An Old School-Fellow," (*Atlantic*, Jan. 1860) described Keats as a pugilist, an association Dickinson was to draw in her poem "A little East of Jordan" (59) and in a letter written late in life which ended with the line " 'Pugilist and Poet, Jacob was correct.' " Joseph Severn's "On the Vicissitudes of Keats's Fame," (*Atlantic*, April 1863) also apparently affected Dickinson. Over twenty years later, she wrote of the death of her friend and fellow author, Helen Hunt Jackson, "Oh had that Keats a Sev-

The Poet's Romance

> You know I'd sooner be a clapping Bell
> To some Kamtschatcan Missionary Church,
> Than with these horrid moods be left i' the lurch.

He would rather be banished to the most remote outpost in the Siberian north; he would prefer to be a "clapping bell," than suffer the aftermath of the destructive vision of cruelty within the sea—awareness carries with it the possibility of despair. The extremity of the image along with the deflating final rhyme mocks as it underscores the pain of Keats's preceding gloomy vision. In his attempt to cheer the ailing Reynolds, Keats discovers that he has written of his own nightmare vision with a too vivid clarity. And at this moment, he would willingly relinquish his own intense observation. Dickinson succumbs to the same emotion, wishing to abandon her role as poet, preferring instead to be the ear which listens.[99] But she realizes, as does Keats, that such an abdication of responsibility commands its own sacrifice. She responds to the self-generated demands placed upon her but refuses to ignore her grim vision of the natural world. She knows that "Narcotics cannot still the Tooth / That nibbles at the soul—."[100] If courage fails, one must overcome it.

> If your Nerve, deny you—
> Go above your Nerve—
> He can lean against the Grave,
> If he fear to swerve— (292)

When she faces the death that haunts her dread of process, Dickinson stands erect; the need to confront her version of reality precludes any desire to defend her bruised spirit. Although both Keats and Dickinson are tempted to relinquish

---

ern!" In *Aurora Leigh*, Elizabeth Barrett Browning praised Keats as the man who, ". . . turning grandly on his central self, / Ensphered himself in twenty perfect years" (Bk. I, 1030-33). James Russell Lowell, Leigh Hunt, Thomas De Quincey, and William Hazlitt all had published essays on Keats included in books owned by the Dickinson Family.

[99] See Dickinson, Poem 505.   [100] Dickinson, Poem 501.

their roles as poets, although both reject the artificial numbing of narcosis, they offer distinct versions of how to cope with the reality they experience. David Perkins suggests that Keats felt, "when dealing with sickness, sorrow, and the like, that he should transmute it into forms which openly offer pleasure and release to the imagination."[101] What he wishes to do through his art he is tempted to do for himself. As Perkins states: ". . . like Wordsworth, he certainly felt the attraction of whatever might deaden feeling and awareness and so mitigate the pain of loss. Throughout his poetry such symbols of Death, Sleep, Lethe and Wine suggest the pull of 'forgetfulness divine,' of an 'age so shelter'd . . . that I may never know how change the moons.' "[102]

Part of the attractiveness of the lover-goddess for Keats lies in the "hope to go beyond time into an intensity which is timeless."[103] Similarly the freedom this dream provides offers Keats the possibility of abandoning the strictures of a painful reality. At moments of happiness he experiences a state somewhere between wakefulness and sleep. He asks, "Was it a vision, or a waking dream?"[104] But each of these altered states of consciousness is only a temporary solution to the problematic reality of the poet's daylight hours. Although Keats continues his quest for unconsciousness, a numbness that will "take away the pain of existence," he repeatedly acknowledges the impossibility of such a state of oblivion.[105] Death, which brings a release from suffering, is a seductive figure, but he is also, alas, the ultimate silencer:

Land and sea, weakness and decline, are great separators, but
Death is the great divorcer forever. . . .[106]

---

[101] Perkins, p. 192.   [102] Ibid., p. 202.   [103] Ibid., p. 222.

[104] Happiness is too mild a word for the momentary *ecstasis* Keats experiences in the "Ode To A Nightingale." He is, ever briefly, literally beside himself, for a sublime instant surrounded by anxiety and regret.

[105] See Morris Dickstein, *Keats and His Poetry: A Study in Development* (Chicago: University of Chicago Press, 1971), p. 12.

[106] See James Russell Lowell, "Keats," in *Among My Books: Second Series*

The Poet's Romance

The process of soul-making is a difficult one; however, Keats rejects any lasting solution that might mitigate his pain at the expense of his voice.

Assessing his life, Keats distinguishes the achieved individual from the mass surrounding him: "There may be intelligences or sparks of the divinity in millions—but they are not Souls [the] till they acquire identities, till each one is personally itself. I[n]telligences are atoms of perception—they know and they see and they are pure, in short they are God—".[107] This is precisely Dickinson's appraisal of the one she most respects:

> Of all the Souls that stand create—
> I have elected—One—
> When Sense from Spirit—files away—
> And Subterfuge—is done—
> When that which is—and that which was—
> Apart—intrinsic—stand—
> And this brief Tragedy of Flesh—
> Is shifted—like a Sand—
> When Figures show their royal Front—
> And Mists—are carved away,
> Behold the Atom—I preferred—
> To all the lists of Clay! (664)

But the formation of such a living "atom" is a tortuous process. In *The Fall of Hyperion*, the poet fights for his life on the lowest step of the altar before the baffling high priestess Moneta. He must mount the first step before the "gummed leaves of sacrifice are burnt," or he will die.

(Boston: Houghton Mifflin and Company, 1876), p. 319. There remains a possibility that Dickinson read Lowell's essay. She comments to Higginson on his review of the book in the March *Scribner's* of 1876, and she scissors a reference to the text. See Leyda, *Years and Hours of Emily Dickinson*, II, p. 244 and Dickinson's *Letters*, letter no. 457, II, 551, Spring 1876, to T. W. Higginson.

[107] Keats, *Letters*, letter no. 159, II, 102, 21 April 1819, to the George Keatses.

The Poet's Romance

> Prodigious seem'd the toil; the leaves were yet
> Burning—when suddenly a palsied chill
> Struck from the paved level up my limbs,
> And was ascending quick to put cold grasp
> Upon those streams that pulse beside the throat:
> I shriek'd, and the sharp anguish of my shriek
> Stung my own ears—I strove hard to escape
> The numbness; strove to gain the lowest step.[108]

Dickinson recalls in "It was not Death, for I stood up," a similar sensation—the frost of burning flesh—the numb, marble feet of paralysis:

> . . . .
> It was not Frost, for on my Flesh
> I felt Siroccos—crawl—
> Nor Fire—for just my Marble feet
> Could keep a Chancel, cool—
> . . . .(510)

What Dickinson faces is not a step into renewed life pouring "in at the toes," but a numbing that does not allow even the possibility of safety or escape. The ceremonies of the altar, "the Chancel," indicate that the moment is sacramental; however, it is not a time of redemption but of all-consuming, unredeemed despair. Life stops, a shock not of death, but of a death in life that cannot or will not cease. The end of Dickinson's poem is desperation. Space itself "stares all around"; this paralysis is "most, like Chaos—Stopless—cool—" with nothing to repeal it. Not even hope enters here—a hope that would at least allow one to experience despair.[109] The sensations Keats undergoes as he struggles upon the first stair Dickinson experiences in the after-life of the survivor, in the numbness that precedes mourning. Keats mounts the stair and steps over the threshold just in time to

---

[108] Keats, *The Fall of Hyperion: A Dream*, see Canto I, ll. 121-128.
[109] See Dickinson, Poem 510.

be saved from death. At her moment of severe testing, however, Dickinson may be seen to hesitate. And, as Geoffrey Hartman suggests, such a pause "extends the liminal moment. The poet's minutes are our days and hours. She chooses to remain *in extremis.* . . ." "She is carried off, perhaps, but she does not give herself." "Her fate is to stay profane, outside the gates, though in sight of the promised land."[110] What she fears is the finality of death, the ultimate silence of the inevitable. The "fact of beauty" and its assured end cannot be severed. Yet she must reject the final step that alone will answer the questions that obsess her. Death is the other side of the liminal moment before which she hesitates. Though she cries, "Beauty crowds me till I die," she does not choose death nor take the final step of accepting life's process. And it is here that Dickinson swerves most decisively from Keats, who wins from himself an acceptance of the essential relation of beauty to death. Although art may create truth in a world of perpetual renewal, in the calm bliss of eternal desire, life offers a different and necessary experience—the limits of mortality are the requisite condition for a humane beauty. Keats's "poem of the earth" breeds a warm acceptance of the conditions of life as he acknowledges that melancholy dwells with a "beauty that must die."

Yet, both Keats and Dickinson keep brooding upon the silence of death, the space after lips are sealed. And both poets express their ambivalence toward the dread suitor who brings release from the pain of life at the price of the final silencing of the poet's voice. As death is, for Keats, the "great Divorcer," so Dickinson sees it in terms of a dissolving marriage.

> Those who have been in the Grave the longest—
> Those who begin Today—
> Equally perish from our Practise—
> Death is the other way—

---

[110] Geoffrey Hartman, *Beyond Formalism* (New Haven: Yale University Press, 1970), pp. 349-351.

The Poet's Romance

> Foot of the Bold did least attempt it—
> It—is the White Exploit—
> Once to achieve, annuls the power
> Once to communicate— (922)

"Annuls" recalls the marriage metaphor as it destroys it. It is "death's finger" which "claps [her] murmuring lip!"[111] About the approaching dissolution of her marriage with words, Dickinson writes:

> Silence is all we dread.
> There's Ransom in a Voice—
> But Silence is Infinity.
> Himself have not a face. (1251)

Death cuts her off from the voices of those she loves and will sever her own ties with the living. Fear of separation joins with a sense of horror at the thought that she will be deprived of the ability to communicate, that the voice of the poet will be silenced. What Keats, however, most fears is his failure to hear, the power of death to interrupt the fluent voice of nature. Thus he too would wish to escape the pain of life but not relinquish life itself. In the "Ode to a Nightingale," he yearns to become one with the bird, borne on the wings of an intoxicated spirit. He would escape the "weariness, the fever, and the fret" of mortal life without embracing death itself. He woos death but knows the sacrifice that dying would demand. Drawn toward death, Keats envisions dying as an ecstasy if he can "cease upon the midnight with no pain," while listening to the voice of the sublime nightingale. Yet, in the very process of describing this moment, Keats turns ecstasy to lament, for the voice he now hears would become silence as he would in death no longer be able to hear it. With this awareness, the poem moves away from a longing for death to a more profound rejection of it.[112] Keats envies the bird because its song is immortal, but his

[111] Dickinson, Poem 56. [112] See *ibid.*, VI, 11. 1-10.

The Poet's Romance

moment of union with it fades as the conditions of mortality reassert themselves. If Keats mourns the future loss of his ability to witness nature, Dickinson rebels against the loss of her own voice. Whereas he incorporates awareness of death into a rounded perception of immediate experience, an informed acceptance of the boundaries as well as the sublimity of existence (his last poems forming a paean to "things as they are"), Dickinson rejects such a resolution.[113] Instead of cohering, her antithetical perception of life splits further apart. Beauty pushes her toward the mystery of immortality, or what she called her "flood subject":

> Beauty crowds me till I die
> Beauty mercy have on me
> But if I expire to-day
> Let it be in sight of thee—(1654)

Paradoxically, because her experience of Beauty is so intense, she must beg for mercy; for she would not want to die without it. Despite this apprehension, Dickinson shares with Keats a refusal to cut off any part of experience, to deny either the conditions of life or the reality of death. She echoes Keats's priorities of religion and love, his sense of vocation, his overwhelming desire to be a poet; but she must leave him as he turns toward a more open, humanistic acceptance of the conditions of life. Thus Dickinson refuses to embrace Keats's hard-won vision, for she prefers to remain in the dark—still questioning, torn by doubt.

In an early, now famous poem, Dickinson sketched a postmortem interview:

> I died for Beauty—but was scarce
> Adjusted in the Tomb
> When One who died for Truth, was lain
> In an adjoining Room—

---

[113] See Wallace Stevens, "The Man With the Blue Guitar," *The Collected Poems of Wallace Stevens* (New York: Alfred A. Knopf, 1978), I, 1. 6, p. 165.

The Poet's Romance

> He questioned softly 'Why I failed'?
> 'For Beauty', I replied—
> 'And I—for Truth—Themself are One—
> We Brethren, are', He said—
>
> And so, as Kinsmen, met a Night—
> We talked between the Rooms—
> Until the Moss had reached our lips—
> And covered up—our names— (449)

She talks with her "brother" between the rooms, two who "fail" because they sacrifice themselves to a beauty and truth that can survive only in the province of art. This is, however, a double failure, for not only have they died, but their names will not live after them as the obliterating moss destroys the possibility that they will be remembered for their sacrifice. Here Dickinson's vision reveals her image of a mythic Keats—one who had met with misunderstanding and incurred the ire of critics, one who died before his poetic promise could be fully realized. But this myth of the failed young poet may be closer to her own sense of loss than to his. For, she saw in him the inner division, the insistence upon integrity, and the antithetical vision that describes her own work. But she could not find there what she did not already possess. Thus she turns away from Keats at the vital moment that marks his triumph—his acceptance of human life, whose loveliness depends upon its limitations. Both Keats and Dickinson, as we have seen, perceive antithetically, and both fall "half in love with easeful Death," but from these mutual perceptions a fissure forms that cannot be bridged.[114] While Keats turns to write the great hymns of the earth, Dickinson continues to war with the enemy of her perceptions. In Keats's poems, Dickinson discovers the "woe of extasy" whose crisis he penetrates to attain his own more conciliatory vision of art. She stops at the threshold, however, in defiance.[115]

[114] Keats, "Ode To A Nightingale," VI, 1. 2.
[115] Dickinson, Poem 1622 (alternative reading for line 4 of poem); see also prose fragment 65, *Letters*, II, 921.

IV

Word and World in Shelley and Dickinson

Dazzling and tremendous how quick the sun-rise would kill me,
If I could not now and always send sun-rise out of me.
                                                —Walt Whitman

DICKINSON redefines nature according to her priorities. The extent to which the exclusive self shapes images around its singular demands informs her distinctive use of language. Although she cannot completely dissolve the relation between word and world, Dickinson does test the limits to which such a process may go. When the ties between nature and the imagination are severed, natural images necessarily achieve a peculiar status, for they no longer depend upon external reality as their source, but rather adhere increasingly to the life within the imagination.[1] Shelley, whose own vi-

---

[1] Commenting on the emergence of the image as "the most prominent dimension of the Romantic style," Paul de Man remarks: "An abundant imagery coinciding with an equally abundant quantity of natural objects, the theme of imagination linked closely to the theme of nature, such is the fundamental ambiguity that characterizes the poetics of romanticism. The tension between the two polarities never ceases to be problematic." (Paul de Man, "Intentional Structure of the Romantic Image," *Romanticism and Consciousness: Essays in Criticism*, ed. Harold Bloom [New York: W. W. Norton & Co., Inc., 1970], p. 66.) It is here within this problematic tension between polarities of natural object and imagination, that Dickinson strives toward the redefinition of the "image" by asserting its ontological status above any external source.

Both Roland Hagenbüchle and Robert Weisbuch have, in different ways, described Dickinson's concept of figural language. Writing from a structuralist point of view, Hagenbüchle terms Dickinson's self-referential image a "transcend": "While the range of meaning of a symbol finds its limits in the concrete object, the transcend remains essentially indeterminate. Outward reality is, so we have found, more and more 'bracketed,' and the only focus

Word and World

sion of the ontological priority of the imagination—the Intellectual Spirit—carries this autonomy furthest among the Romantics, is in this regard Dickinson's most powerful forebear. Examining Dickinson's figural language against Shelley's thus serves to clarify the origins of her linguistic experiments as well as to offer a way to assess the effects on her poetry of her determination to intensify the Romantics' growing emphasis upon the autonomy of the working imagination. Such a process of radical internalization is, of course, not without its difficulties. Consequently, Dickinson's images betray ambivalence; for nature may rebel against the poet's ambitions, proving that it possesses a power equal to her own. This drama of internalization, a struggle for priority and control over the origins of the image, determines Dickinson's use of astronomical language. Lightning, for example, may reflect the requirements of the solipsistic self, or, on the other hand, discharge a power issuing from a resentful nature or an immune deity. Thus, the status of Dickinson's natural images shifts as she enacts the appropriation of the natural world into the sovereign self.

Reading Dickinson over against Shelley, briefly tracking their choice of language and comparing their use of apoca-

---

where the relations still meet is finally the poet's consciousness." (Roland Hagenbüchle, "Precision and Indeterminacy in the Poetry of Emily Dickinson," *ESQ: A Journal of the American Renaissance* [Pullman, Washington: Washington State University Press], volume 20, 1st Quarter 1974, p. 43.)

Weisbuch sees Dickinson's poems as participating in a "major romantic form" which he identifies as "anti-allegory." Because his definition is very much to the point here, I repeat it (see Introduction, note 10):

"Anti-allegories often pose as heuristic allegories, as a series of events, scenes, and attitudes in search of an abstract, referential explanation. Because their situations are clearly illustrative and appear potentially encyclopedic, anti-allegories are, in a broad sense, allegorical. They force the reader to seek out causal implications. In search of them, the reader looks to see where the language points, to which authoritative orders. In fact, he may find in the poem many gestures toward such orders, but finally he is forced back by this very plethora of suggestion from a monistic, referential interpretation, forced back to a holistic description of the poem's pattern in terms of nothing but itself." (Robert Weisbuch, *Emily Dickinson's Poetry* [Chicago and London: The University of Chicago Press, 1975], p. 48.)

lyptic images, I suggest that these poets share a fundamental conception of the high ambitions of the Word, that both strive to wipe out the figural aspect of language, attempting to destroy, in the process, the need for metaphoricity itself. What J. Hillis Miller says of Shelley applies, with even more force, to Dickinson. Shelley seeks, according to Miller, a "performative apocalypse in which words will become the fire they have ignited and so vanish as words, in a universal light. The words, however, always remain, there on the page, as the unconsumed traces of each unsuccessful attempt to use words to end words."[2] Pursuing a related apocalypse of language, Dickinson invokes images that describe natural catastrophe—lightning, earthquake, astronomical collisions—to articulate her desire to convert the word from its function as sign to the status of the signified. Naturally, such a desire cannot be fulfilled if poetry is to survive. By tying externally derived images to self-reflexive meanings, however, Dickinson moves toward creating a more radically private figural mode than does Shelley, a mode that attests to the primacy of the isolated imagination. Thus, she extends and intensifies Shelley's quest by converting the image, which for Shelley is the trace of failure (sign that he has failed to transcend language) into the Sacred Word. In terms of poetics, the Word for Dickinson becomes transubstantiated, becomes the thing itself. Although no human poet can ever convert word into living thing, this is Dickinson's high ambition and her most radical experiment in language. Not unexpectedly, when the Word is made flesh, Dickinson appropriates the vocabulary of the Sacred to herself: She writes;

. . . .
A Word that breathes distinctly
Has not the power to die
Cohesive as the Spirit

[2] J. Hillis Miller, "The Critic as Host," *Deconstruction & Criticism* (New York: A Continuum Book, The Seabury Press, 1979), p. 237. For a brilliant discussion of Shelley based on this premise, see Miller, pp. 232-252.

Word and World

> It may expire if He—
> 'Made Flesh and dwelt among us
> Could condescension be
> Like this consent of Language
> This loved Philology (1651)

The competition between Christ's love and Philology ends in her choosing the consent of language. Appropriating theological language to her alternative poetics, Dickinson signals her antinomian intent. The poet's Word displaces the Christian *Logos*, as power inheres within. Yet Dickinson does not, for she cannot, abandon the language of the world which remains, after all, the language of poetry. Instead, she uses cosmological phenomena, which express their alternative allegiance to and origins in her consciousness as it quests for a release from the merely natural.

I open this intrapoetic investigation with a discussion of the individual words Dickinson discovers in Shelley and her transfer of them to her own ground; I then proceed to more complex images, ways of seeing, which Dickinson shares with Shelley but lends her distinct "slant."[3] An examination of a few passages from Shelley's longer poems illustrates, moreover, how Dickinson asserts control over her precursor's language and clarifies the relation between her poems and Shelley's "italic seed."[4] Yet, the choice of her word and its sanctification do not diminish, but rather intensify the sense of ambivalence or anxiety surrounding such a deliberately anti-natural activity. It is no surprise, therefore, that Dickinson conceives of the act of writing a poem as a highly charged event. The struggle to be a poet and the moment of writing the poem are one of her main subjects, a process she describes in cosmic language which strengthens the analogue between the poet confronting internal consciousness and the self facing nature. Lightning may strike, but it is an extra-natural fork—both sign and agent of its potency:

[3] See Dickinson, Poem 1129.   [4] See Dickinson, Poem 945.

Word and World

>. . . . .
> Omnipotence—had not a Tongue—
> His lisp—is Lightning—and the Sun—
> His Conversation—with the Sea—
> 'How shall you know'?
> Consult your Eye! (420)

The immediate presence that cannot be denied, the omnipotence of the irrevocable flash, are the signal proof of how one knows. And yet this lightning is unique; it is not simply the electric, occasional bolt of a summer thunderstorm, for it adheres to consciousness and achieves an identity beyond the merely natural.

> It struck me—every Day—
> The Lightning was as new
> As if the Cloud that instant slit
> And let the Fire through—
> . . . . (362)

All that we know of the turmoil which causes such pain is the character of the image with which Dickinson describes it. Lightning no longer conforms to our expectations but instead assumes properties that originate in the poet's imaginal experience. It singles out the poet and "burns" her in the night while she is sleeping; this "natural" force "blisters" *to* her dream, as if she were the cause of its renewed severity—a private lightning that *depends* upon the power of its constant victim for its own destructive vitality. Yet, characteristically, lightning bestows on the self a power for which there is no recompense; "But I would not exchange the Bolt / For all the rest of Life—" (1581)

This vision of lightning's striking its perpetually grateful victim refers, as I have mentioned earlier, to Dickinson's conception of both poetic inspiration and love.

> To pile like Thunder to it's close
> Then crumble grand away

Word and World

> While Everything created hid
> This—would be Poetry—
>
> Or Love—the two coeval come—
> We both and neither prove—
> Experience either and consume—
> For None see God and live— (1247)

The ability to sound and to reverberate like thunder transforms itself into the voice of the poet branding her for love.

Dickinson's copy of Webster's Dictionary defines lightning as "1. A sudden discharge of electricity from a cloud to the earth, or from the earth to a cloud, or from one cloud to another, that is, from a body positively charged to one negatively charged, producing a vivid flash of light, and usually a loud report, called thunder."[5] The "loud report" resulting from the electric infusion of a positively charged being into a negatively charged self signifies for Dickinson the destructive yet necessary relation between the bestower of the poetic voice and its astonished ephebe. When Dickinson asserts she would rather be passive audience than active poet, she clinches her argument by invoking the dread power of self-inflicted lightning,

> . . . .
> A privilege so awful
> What would the Dower be,
> Had I the Art to Stun myself
> With Bolts of Melody! (505)

The "I" apparently rejects such powers because the sacrifice required to attain them, the "dower" given to the bridegroom of the potent, masculine self, would be immense. Instead she embraces the subordinate position of receptive ad-

---

[5] The edition of the dictionary Dickinson used was Noah Webster, *An American Dictionary of the English Language* (Amherst, Massachusetts, 1844). This is now in the Houghton Library's collection of the Dickinson Family books and contains the autograph of Edward Dickinson and the date, 1847.

mirer just as she invokes the "awe" she must reject. The bolt itself "singes" the melody, obviating the need for a responsive, thunderous voice. In the meantime, Dickinson *has*, ironically, written her poem, drawing on the very poetic powers she has vowed to eschew.

Lightning, however, means more than the bolt of poetic election; it illumines the self's relation to awe, to a life beyond the mortal which must finally remain invisible:

> The Soul's distinct connection
> With immortality
> Is best disclosed by Danger
> Or quick Calamity—
>
> As Lightning on a Landscape
> Exhibits Sheets of Place—
> Not yet suspected—but for Flash—
> And Click—and Suddenness. (974)

Moments of danger or calamity shock us into an awareness of our connection with "immortality," here a trope for death; moments, Dickinson tells us, akin to the vision in a flash of lightning—a vision not even thought of but for the brief flash that renders the invisible known. This sudden vision, however, reveals danger, and Dickinson realizes the need to protect the self against the blinding effect of these flashes, instructive yet potentially damaging. If Dickinson experiences the creative act as threatening, so the force of language itself must be guarded with care lest it sear its reader-victims.

> Tell all the Truth but tell it slant—
> Success in Circuit lies
> Too bright for our infirm Delight
> The Truth's superb surprise
> As Lightning to the Children eased
> With explanation kind
> The Truth must dazzle gradually
> Or every man be blind— (1129)

The method of art should be modified so as not to blind the reader, who requires protection from the destructive power of "truth," the originating experience preserved in the searing image of the lightning bolt. Dickinson diminishes and thus paradoxically strengthens the horror of the lightning in a single, urbane gesture; she domesticates the "nearness to tremendousness," and at once demeans the natural fact as she assigns to it its own peculiar horror:

> The Lightning is a yellow Fork
> From Tables in the sky
> By inadvertent fingers dropt
> The awful Cutlery
>
> Of mansions never quite disclosed
> And never quite concealed
> The Apparatus of the Dark
> To ignorance revealed. (1173)

Again, the carelessness of the Divine diner only partially reveals to the ignorant the mansions of the sky. The destructive potential which results from his casually dropping the "fork," a slight domestic accident, becomes the crucial fact in a human life, yet another instance of the effect unknown powers can have on the self.

If Shelley and Dickinson assert the power of the autonomous imagination, so they both invest astronomical forces with ambivalence, intensity, and a lethal potency. Shelley's lightning, for instance, is one of complex powers, a force that in its various appearances resembles Dickinson's. In "The Triumph of Life," Bacon's eagle spirit leaps "Like lightning out of darkness"; he compels nature to reveal its secrets, illuminated by the lightning of the human, soaring spirit.[6] Here Shelley associates lightning with the power of man, and this vision of ambiguously potent natural forces, which he uses for his own purposes, recalls Dickinson's im-

[6] See Percy Bysshe Shelley, "The Triumph of Life," 11. 266-273. The edition of Shelley's poetry used throughout this chapter is *Shelley: Poetical Works*, ed. Thomas Hutchinson (London: Oxford University Press, 1967).

ages of light. Reading these poets through each other, one discovers not simply the range of their shared vocabulary but, more importantly, their related yet distinct conceptions of a powerful, responsive cosmology. Shelley's vision of an active, violent natural world swirling into and out of storms is the basis for his individual images. We think, for a moment, of a Van Gogh sky—a scene of continuous movement and constant circular becoming. When Shelley projects a reciprocity between the powers of man and nature in one encompassing cosmic metaphor, he moves closer to Dickinson's brand of lightning. First, in "Adonais," Shelley invokes lightning to identify it with the brilliance of the "Pilgrim of Eternity" (Byron), who, mourning the death of Keats, veils "all the lightnings of his song / In sorrow."[7] In *Epipsychidion*, "true love" "overleaps all fence: / Like lightning, with invisible violence / Piercing its continents."[8] Most importantly, however, Shelley associates lightning with the power of the imagination itself which destroys "Error," the worm, the greater phallic potency wiping out this relatively puny earthbound creature:

> 'tis like thy light,
> *Imagination!* which from earth and sky,
> And from the depths of human fantasy,
> As from a thousand prisms and mirrors, fills
> The Universe with glorious beams, and kills
> Error, the worm, with many a sun-like arrow
> Of its reverberating lightning.[9]

Here Shelley conceives of the light of the imagination as a necessary, defensive power in the war between Error and the imagination. The power of explosive thrust with its destructive energy is not confined to the sky but emerges from within the earth itself. Thus, the volcanoes which smoulder and erupt in Shelley's poems find their descendants in Dick-

---

[7] Shelley, "Adonais," XXX, 11. 267-268.
[8] Shelley, *Epipsychidion*, 11. 398-400.
[9] *Ibid.*, 11. 163-169.

inson's landscape—but with a single difference: she once again converts Shelley's apocalyptic mountains into a private symbol of the self.[10] The oral power of the poet becomes at once potentially destructive and intensely pleasurable, for its origins lie, as Adrienne Rich has remarked, in Dickinson's ambivalent "relationship to her own power." Volcanoes, Dickinson contends, need not be sought in remote regions, for one exists in the neighborhood of the self: "A Crater I may contemplate / Vesuvius at Home" (1705). The potential devastation of a "still—Volcano—life" conveys with appropriate conviction Dickinson's fear of her own voice's power.[11] The need to suppress, to work in secret and "under cover," finds adequate representation in the volcano. As Rich remarks, "the woman who feels herself to be Vesuvius at home has need of a mask, at least of inocuousness and of containment."[12] Shelley's volcanoes, which erupt with apocalyptic power at his will, retain, however, the aspect of external images of the soaring "oracular vapour" of the universe, only secondarily echoing private upheaval or social revolution.[13] The volcano's voice roars through the cosmos:

'And that slaughter to the Nation
Shall steam up like inspiration,

[10] Throughout *Epipsychidion*, Shelley links external natural images with the life of the soul. He couples words to the effect of lightning (11. 33-34):

Ay, even the dim words which obscure thee now
Flash, lightning-like, with unaccustomed glow; . . .

And he internalizes the force of lightning to describe the depths within the self (11. 89-90):

Under the lightnings of the soul—too deep—
For the brief fathom-line of thought or sense.

[11] See my discussion of volcanic imagery on pp. 49-50.
[12] See Adrienne Rich, "Vesuvius at Home: The Power of Emily Dickinson," *Shakespeare's Sisters: Feminist Essays on Women Poets*, ed. Sandra M. Gilbert and Susan Gubar. (Bloomington and London: Indiana University Press, 1979), pp. 105, 108, and *passim*.
[13] Shelley, *Prometheus Unbound*, II, iii, 4.

Word and World

> Eloquent, oracular;
> A volcano heard afar.[14]

Its fires burst in fluent streams:

> We had soared beneath these mountains
> Unresting ages; nor had thunder,
> Nor yon volcano's flaming fountains,
> Nor any power above or under
> Ever made us mute with wonder.[15]

The light of the volcano overwhelms, for only liberty surpasses the "type" of dazzling brightness: "thy stare / Makes blind the volcanoes: . . . ."[16] Destructive lava spews out over the land:

> Among those mighty towers and
>   fanes
> Dropped fire, as a volcano rains
> Its sulphurous ruin on the plains.[17]

This oracular, streaming symbol of earthly destruction becomes for Dickinson a symbol of the power of language, the push of the word.[18] Although Dickinson has never seen "volcanoes," she describes their power in personal terms:

> . . . .
> If the stillness is Volcanic
> In the human face
> When upon a pain Titanic
> Features keep their place—

---

[14] Shelley, *The Mask of Anarchy*, LXXXIX, 360-363.
[15] Shelley, *Prometheus Unbound*, I, 86-90.
[16] Shelley, "Liberty," III, 14-15.
[17] Shelley, "Marianne's Dream," XII, 75-77.
[18] For a discussion of the possible psychoanalytic implications of this imagery see Cody, *After Great Pain*, p. 408.

Word and World

> If at length, the smouldering anguish
> Will not overcome—
> And the palpitating Vineyard
> In the dust, be thrown?
>
> If some loving Antiquary,
> On Resumption Morn,
> Will not cry with joy 'Pompeii'!
> To the Hills return! (175)

The vineyards may, indeed, be thrust to ruin; yet, when the volcano erupts, it experiences the intense pleasure of release.[19] In "My Life had stood—a Loaded Gun—," the smile of such pleasure bathes the valley beneath in its "cordial" deathly illumination:

> And do I smile, such cordial light
> Upon the Valley glow—
> It is as a Vesuvian face
> Had let it's pleasure through— (754)

Repeatedly, Dickinson acknowledges the potential horror of

> . . . .
> The Solemn—Torrid—Symbol—
> The lips that never lie—
> Whose hissing Corals part—and shut—
> And Cities—ooze away— (601)

Whether in Shelley or in Emerson—another predecessor here—Dickinson finds in the dialectical image of their volcanoes violent possibilities for pleasure and pain which she internalizes and then converts to her own extra-natural purposes.[20]

---

[19] For a discussion of Dickinson's volcanic imagery in relation to Emerson, see the following chapter, pp. 176-177.

[20] For an evaluation of Emerson's reaction to Shelley, see Julia Power's

Word and World

Dickinson's conversion of natural phenomena is, however, partly anticipated in Shelley. For example, using the image of the hunt, especially its climactic moments to describe his own sense of internal terror, Shelley assumes the *persona* of a wounded prey pursued by ruthless hounds.

> . . . and now he fled astray
> With feeble steps o'er the world's wilderness,
> And his own thoughts, along that rugged way,
> Pursued, like raging hounds, their father and their prey.[21]

The beasts, his thoughts, turn against their own source, the father who becomes a victim of what he himself has engendered.[22] But Dickinson further transforms this image of the victim into a self who regards the single hound not simply as a threat but as her necessary, indeed sole companion:[23]

> This Consciousness that is aware
> Of Neighbors and the Sun
> Will be the one aware of Death
> And that itself alone
>
> Is traversing the interval
> Experience between
> And most profound experiment
> Appointed unto Men—
>
> How adequate unto itself
> It's properties shall be

Shelley in America in the Nineteenth Century: His Relation to American Critical Thought and Influence (New York: Gordian Press, 1969).

[21] Shelley, "Adonais," XXXI, 11. 276-279.

[22] Earl R. Wasserman in his *Shelley: A Critical Reading* (Baltimore: The Johns Hopkins Press, 1971), p. 502, suggests that in this passage from "Adonais," Shelley is preparing for the identification of himself with Keats: ". . . and just as Adonis-Adonais was slain by a boar, so Shelley is an Actaeon being destroyed by his own hounds, which are 'his own thoughts.' "

[23] For another discussion of this poem, see Harold Bloom, "Death and the Native Strain in American Poetry," in *Death In American Experience*, ed. Arien Mack (New York: Schocken Books, 1973), pp. 83-96.

Word and World

> Itself unto itself and none
> Shall make discovery.
>
> Adventure most unto itself
> The Soul condemned to be—
> Attended by a single Hound
> It's own identity. (822)

The "totemic hound," as Harold Bloom calls him, is consciousness, the identity of the self, both an adequate and essential companion to the traversing Soul. Having lost the stigma of the devouring brute, he attends, waits upon, and accompanies the traveller. And yet another meaning resides within the word, for the voyager is "hounded" by consciousness; it could not escape its sole companion even if it so desired. Ambivalence exists within the possible meanings of the single hound, an ambivalence Dickinson continues to exploit with assurance.

If Shelley repeatedly identifies the pursued deer as a symbol of personal persecution, Dickinson adopts a related identification, finding within the terror of the pursuit the potential for an heroic cry that rises from the struggle:[24]

> A *Wounded* Deer—leaps highest—
> I've heard the Hunter tell—
> 'Tis but the Extasy of *death*—
> And then the Brake is still!
> . . . . (165)

The extra push of strength derives from mortal extremity as pressure provokes the heightened response that deludes the observer. The desire to maintain "face," to betray reality in order to keep up appearances, lies at the core of such courage. If the "worst" has the salutary effect of evoking the

---

[24] For a more general comparison between Shelley's and Dickinson's use of the image of the hunted deer see Dickinson, poems 165, 186, 565, 842, 979, and Shelley's "Orpheus," "The Cenci," I, ii, 11-13, *Epipsychidion*, 271-276, and "To Edward Williams," 2-3.

Word and World

"best" in response, it has an additional advantage as well, for it provides a certain immunity, the assurance that when the worst is met, the self wins a reprieve; it cannot come again. Once wounded, the deer no longer protests; as victim, the self has lost its attraction for the pursuer:

> . . . .
> The Maimed may pause, and breathe,
> And glance securely round—
> The Deer attracts no further
> Than it resists—the Hound— (979)[25]

Drawing upon a related scene, Dickinson envisions the relationship of text and reader in terms of the hunt:

> Good to hide, and hear 'em hunt!
> Better to be found,
> If one care to, that is,
> The Fox fits the Hound—
>
> Good to know, and not tell,
> Best, to know and tell,
> Can one find the rare Ear
> Not too dull— (842)

Adopting a characteristic Shelleyan metaphor, Dickinson here yokes it to her own fears, which recall Shelley's justified anxiety at the opening of *Epipsychidion*:

> My Song, I fear that thou wilt find but few
> Who fitly shall conceive thy reasoning,
> Of such hard matter dost thou entertain.[26]

---

[25] Suggested changes for lines seven and eight read

> 7 attracts no further] invites no longer—
> 8 Than it resists] than it evades— / eludes—

For texts, see Dickinson, Poem 979.

[26] Shelley, *Epipsychidion*, 1-3.

Word and World

INDEED, Dickinson may well have been one of those "rare Ears" that read and reacted so strongly to Shelley's poem, for her close reading of *Epipsychidion* is suggested both by the lines that appear in the margins of her copy of Shelley as well as by a group of her poems belonging to a single packet which appear to use, as their germ, phrases that echo Shelley's poem. *The Poetical Works of Percy Bysshe Shelley* (Philadelphia: Grissy and Markley, 1853), the volume now in the Houghton Library's collection of Dickinson family books, bears the signature of Susan Gilbert and the date, 1854. This copy has marks beside the following poems: "Goodnight," "Mutability," "On a Faded Violet," "The Sensitive Plant," "The Cloud," and "To A Skylark." Each of these poems has an "x" beside it. This edition also has lines beside the following:

> Narrow
> The heart that loves, the brain that contemplates,
> The life that wears, the spirit that creates
> One object, and one form, and builds thereby
> A sepulchre for its eternity. *(Epipsychidion)*

> Many a green isle needs must be
> In the deep wide sea of Misery,
> Or the mariner, worn and wan,
> Never thus could voyage on—
> ("Lines written among the Euganean Hills")

> And with ghastly whispers tell
> That joy, once lost, is pain. ("The Past")

> Art thou pale for weariness
> Of climbing heaven, and gazing on the earth,
> Wandering companionless
> Among the stars that have a different birth,—
> And everchanging, like a joyless eye
> That finds no object worth its constancy?
> ("To the Moon")

Word and World

"The Waning Moon" is enclosed in penciled brackets, and the page is folded back, and there is a mark next to "Ode to Liberty." The corner of the page is also turned down on p. 275, "Ode to the West Wind." Although one cannot be certain that Emily Dickinson is responsible for these marks, the pencil lines beside the passages cited are consistent with those generally thought to be hers. There are light lines drawn next to the passages from these poems. Other books Dickinson is known to have read also contain "x's." Whether, once again, these marks are Dickinson's, Sue's, or someone else's, the reader cannot be absolutely sure. However, the penciled vertical lines are strikingly similar to those found in an edition of Longfellow's *Kavanagh* which, according to Professor Richard Sewall, was Emily Dickinson's copy and is still intact.

The relationship of Dickinson's work to her precursor's, however, is more than one of an apparent borrowing of words, although even on this level a little surmise may be instructive. If she read the lines, "Possessing and possessed by all that is / Within that calm circumference of bliss," one could easily imagine her pleasure at discovering another sense of circumference: of a reciprocal love fulfilled in an earthly sphere, a literal island of bliss.[27] Dickinson takes the image of mutuality, of possessing and possessed, and fuses it to a circumference of her own. In a letter to Daniel Chester French, she congratulates the sculptor on his recently completed statue of John Harvard. She writes:

Dear Mr. French:—
　　We learn with delight of the recent acquisition to your fame, and hasten to congratulate you on an honor so reverently won. Success is dust, but an aim forever touched with dew. God keep you fundamental!

　　　　　Circumference, thou Bride
　　　　　Of awe,—possessing thou

[27] Shelley, *Epipsychidion*, 549-550.

Word and World

> Shalt be possessed by
> Every hallowed knight
> That dares to covet thee.[28]

The four-line poem is preceded by the thought that success crumbles when it is attained, that it is impossible to secure; but the promise of achievement is refreshing and therefore tempts the artist. Whereas the aim, with its power to nurture, offers life, fulfillment is dry as dust. Read in the context of the letter, the poet suggests that Circumference, the unattainable bliss, can be achieved through an implied distance, at the moment of longing when the Knight "dares" desire it. Only in the act of aiming, in the distance of desire, can one approach the impossible. An alternative last line to the poem which Dickinson crossed out, "that bends a knee to thee," emphasizes this distance between the bowing, devotional knight and his desire. But it also echoes Shelley's own closing lines to *Epipsychidion* as Dickinson's poem addresses one of its meanings.

> Weak Verses, go, kneel at your Sovereign's feet,
> And say:—'We are the masters of thy slave;
> What wouldest thou with us and ours and thine?'
> Then call your sisters from Oblivion's cave,
> All singing loud: 'Love's very pain is sweet,
> But its reward is in the world divine
> Which, if not here, it builds beyond the grave.'
> So shall ye live when I am there.[29]

Shelley has sought to resolve the question of whether perfect beauty and complete unity with the Ideal are possible on earth. Despite his momentary promise of an earthly bliss, he remains ultimately defeated and unconvinced. The voices from Oblivion's Cave chant that such fulfillment may follow only after death, and yet Shelley cannot persuade himself

[28] Dickinson, Poem 1620. For the history of the manuscript see Johnson's discussion in III, p. 1112.
[29] Shelley, *Epipsychidion*, 592-599.

completely of a life after death. Such a belief results, he senses, from desire rather than from reason. *Epipsychidion* was, as C. E. Pulos suggests, Shelley's attempt to resolve this dilemma, to seek death because ideal beauty existed there alone. This pursuit conflicts with Shelley's own doubt as to any possibility of an afterlife. As Pulos states, "what he [Shelley] was seeking escape from in 'Epipsychidion'—perhaps without being fully aware of it—was the concentration of hope upon an afterlife about which he knew that he knew nothing."[30] In her letter to French, Dickinson apparently identifies with Shelley's dilemma and presents a response to his crisis. She addresses Shelley's concern and returns to it, taking as her source lines which have an explicitly different meaning in the context of Shelley's poem. The fulfillment she finds so problematic exists, according to Dickinson, in the *desiring* of it; the kind of completion Shelley longs for leads only to dust. But we need to acknowledge that here Dickinson refers not to love, but to a vision of artistic success, although for both poets, the two, as I have earlier suggested, are intimately related.

In another instance of this kind of dialogue, Dickinson apparently drew a line beside:

> Narrow
> The heart that loves, the brain that contemplates,
> The life that wears, the spirit that creates
> One object, and one form, and builds thereby
> A sepulchre for its eternity.[31]

This passage refers to the stifling tomb that one builds for oneself through monogamous marriage, an arrangement that leads to self-created living death. Again Dickinson seems to absorb these lines and formulate her own response to the opening of *Epipsychidion*, which announces the nature of the poet's quest. Shelley writes:

[30] C. E. Pulos, *The Deep Truth: A Study of Shelley's Scepticism* (Lincoln: University of Nebraska Press, 1954), pp. 81-86.
[31] Shelley, *Epipsychidion*, 169-173.

Word and World

> I never thought before my death to see
> Youth's vision thus made perfect. Emily,
> I love thee; though the world by no thin name
> Will hide that love from its unvalued shame.
> Would we two had been twins of the same mother!
> Or, that the name my heart lent to another
> Could be a sister's bond for her and thee,
> Blending two beams of one eternity![32]

Once having caught a glimpse of his ideal "Emily," a name Dickinson may have thought Shelley chose advisedly if not prophetically, he pursues her through the deluding forms of mortal life. At the moment of desperation, he employs the image of a hunted deer, which Dickinson also uses to describe crisis:

> Then, as a hunted deer that could not flee,
> I turned upon my thoughts, and stood at bay,
> Wounded and weak and panting; the cold day
> Trembled, for pity of my strife and pain.
> When, like a noonday dawn, there shone again
> Deliverance.[33]

At his furthest extremity of suffering, the self fulfills if only momentarily and in a dream, his quest, an occasion reminiscent of the pause that redeems the injured deer in Dickinson's poem. Whereas Dickinson's deer achieves a respite from pursuit, Shelley's self realizes his goal only to be deceived by the Spirit of his dream. Dickinson rejects even the possibility of attaining the Ideal in life, and she is equivocal also about the possibility of achieving it after death:

> Till Death—is narrow Loving—
> The scantest Heart extant
> Will hold you till your privilege
> Of Finiteness—be spent—

[32] *Ibid.*, 41-48.   [33] *Ibid.*, 272-277.

Word and World

As she echoes Shelley's attack on monogamy which begins "Narrow / the heart that loves," Dickinson seems to be responding to her precursor's aim throughout the poem. Death itself becomes the crucial and determining factor in the capacity to love, not the poet's death, but the death of the one she loves:

> But He whose loss procures you
> Such Destitution that
> Your Life too abject for itself
> Thenceforward imitate—

It is only through his absence that her imagination can take hold and remake the lover into a being worthy of her complete devotion. In the condition of living, the "scantest heart" will hold her, for the test comes through and by death. The grief one suffers determines the extent of love; one strives to imitate the lost beloved's life because the poet's own has turned worthless through its loss.

> Until—Resemblance perfect—
> Yourself, for His pursuit
> Delight of Nature—abdicate—
> Exhibit Love—somewhat— (907)

"Resemblance perfect" recalls the twin form that Shelley seeks in Emily. And Dickinson here asserts that to make life over in the departed's image, one must relinquish the pleasure of nature, the conditions of the natural world—life itself must be abandoned. Only then, after the death of the beloved and the sacrifice of the natural world, can love appear. Yet the final "somewhat" is a characteristic evasion; Dickinson does not commit herself completely to her version of where the ideal Love can be found, for absence of the lover and the world he has left behind only partially yield to love. The possibility of such commitment depends upon the precondition of death. Dickinson denies the possibility of Shelley's tentative vision as she insists upon the distance he seeks to dissolve. Thus she characteristically reacts to the premises of Shelley's quest by using the germ of his own language to present a negative response to the possibility of achieving an ideal union in life.

On the same sheet of paper as the first draft of "Circumference thou Bride of Awe," Dickinson writes "Arrows enamored of his Heart," which bears a more positive relation to *Epipsychidion*.[34] The impetus for this poem may be the lines that follow the passage which forms the basis for "Circumference thou Bride of Awe." Envisioning his fulfilled love on the "Elysian isle," Shelley imagines that he and Emily are making love in a dark cavern while the noontime sun shines outside their shadow:

> And we will talk, until thought's melody
> Become too sweet for utterance, and it die
> In words, to live again in looks, which dart
> With thrilling tone into the voiceless heart,
> Harmonizing silence without a sound.[35]

Dickinson complicates the Shelleyan process of thoughts "too sweet" for language which are reborn into looks that speak with the directness of darts by suggesting that potentially lethal arrows lose their penetrative force because they love their target, as venoms lose their power for harm because the victim assumes them to be benign. Thus, apparent mutual misunderstanding of antagonistic intentions converts a lethal into a safe relationship:

> Arrows enamored of his Heart—
> Forgot to rankle there
> And Venoms he mistook for Balms
> disdained to rankle there— (1629)

In the margin beside this nearly illegible worksheet draft Dickinson wrote, "reformed to nothing but Delight which

---

[34] See Johnson's note in *Poems*, p. 1112.   [35] *Epipsychidion*, 560-564.

Word and World

..., "[36] perhaps an attempted continuation of this poem or the reworking of "Circumference thou Bride of Awe," or the beginning of a new poem. But the line is important because it echoes yet another from *Epipsychidion*, " . . . henceforth be thou united / Even as a bride, delighting and delighted." Dickinson may be connecting the image of the delighting and delighted bride with the relationship Shelley suggests existed between circumference and awe, two words crucial to her own vocabulary. As Circumference is "possessing and possessed," a condition of reciprocity, so the bride is delighted and also becomes the source of joy—she is delightful to her lover. Dickinson establishes the identity of the relationship and perhaps superimposes the first passage from *Epipsychidion* onto the second to make her poem, "Circumference thou Bride of Awe." She writes a distinct and original poem which banishes the hope at the heart of *Epipsychidion* and, in the process, appropriates several images from Shelley's poem to inform her own ambivalent response. Despite the strong circumstantial evidence for such an interpretation, it must remain conjectural, but whether this is the precise relationship of Dickinson's poem to her source is not the point. What matters is the antithetical freedom with which Dickinson treats words and images to argue against their origins. Thus, a dialogic pattern develops, one that Dickinson sustains throughout her reading not only of Shelley but also of other poets. Evidently, Dickinson felt free to alter received meanings, and even appears to have reformed the language of the precursor poem itself to make clear her own critical reactions to a text. That she exercises such freedom is one of the difficulties a reader faces who might seek to uncover instances of specific influence. What I have traced in the foregoing, however, is a *paradigm of possibility*, one way Dickinson might have used a generative poem to break through to a poem of her own. Repeated instances that reveal a similar relationship between a text and its parent suggest that something akin to this process lies

---

[36] See Johnson's note to Poem 1629.

Word and World

close to her method of writing, and it is in this difficult and shadowy area that we may discover Dickinson's poetic echoes.

ALTHOUGH *Epipsychidion* abounds with images, analogues, and metaphors, this abundance does not seem to have disturbed Dickinson as it has so many other readers before and after her. Instead, *Epipsychidion* appears to have served as an imagistic mine for her own poetry. Among the most compelling examples of the relationship between Shelley's linguistic imagination and Dickinson's response occurs in the imagistic area of "astronomical absorption," by which I mean those images that combine two forces in the sky that merge, fuse, or obliterate one another. The opening of Shelley's poem, a paean to Emily, describes her as a "radiant form";[37] star and moon, her light causes the poet's words to "Flash, lightning-like, with unaccustomed glow."[38] She is lamp, flame, immovable star. When Emily appears as a deer, it is "the brightness / Of her divinest presence" which "trembles through / Her limbs."[39] Her voice resembles "planetary music heard in trance."[40] Literally "heavenly," she is above the poet, and in complete control of his universe, determining the light and darkness of his consciousness. The antithetical force within light can also destroy the vision of the poet as the light's intensity causes Shelley's "moth-like Muse" to burn its wings.[41] The power of the flame acts on life, often for good but with the potential for evil as well. The light of love is like the light of imagination that

>   fills
>   The Universe with glorious beams, and kills
>   Error, the worm, with many a sun-like arrow
>   Of its reverberated lightning.[42]

---

[37] Shelley, *Epipsychidion*, 22.
[38] *Ibid.*, 34.
[39] *Ibid.*, 77-79.
[40] *Ibid.*, 86.
[41] *Ibid.*, 53.
[42] *Ibid.*, 166-169.

Shelley reiterates the essentially self-destructive analogue of the poet's seeking his muse to the moth flying into its fatal flame. He is overcome with vertiginous desire.

One of the earthly, false forms of Emily that the poet meets on his quest breathes "electric poison,—flame / [that] Out of her looks into my vitals came, . . ."[43] The tainted breath of flame is the other side of Emily's divine, life-giving illumination. Suffering because of the absolute power he has bestowed upon his Ideal vision, Shelley renders himself vulnerable through the power he ascribes to her. If she has been described as a trembling antelope, he becomes a trapped and hunted deer, robbed of health, "wounded and weak and panting." It is the "cold day" which trembles this time, "for pity" of his "strife and pain";[44] what saves him he perceives as light:

> When, like a noonday dawn, there shone again
> Deliverance.[45]

This time it is the "cold chaste moon" devoid of the passionate flame that carries him through the dream of crisis to his beloved. His crisis, however, affects the guiding moon as well, for it shrinks "as in the sickness of eclipse" to witness the return of his lost vision.[46] Her "splendour" also is like "the Morn's."[47] "And from her presence life was radiated."[48] Her light carries a piercing force:

> I stood, and felt the dawn of my long night
> Was penetrating me with living light: . . .[49]

This conjunction of illumination, life-giving warmth, and the penetrative force of light combines with the power of the nurturing female who bears the food of life; Emily becomes both the lost sister-soul (the poet's twin) and mother. He

---

[43] *Ibid.*, 259-260. [44] *Ibid.*, 275.
[45] *Ibid.*, 276-277. [46] *Ibid.*, 310.
[47] *Ibid.*, 324. [48] *Ibid.*, 325.
[49] *Ibid.*, 341-342.

wishes her to be vestal sister and bride—the chaste image Dickinson avowed for herself. Yet love manifests its destructive force once more; it is "Like lightning . . . like Heaven's free breath, . . . liker Death," for it has the capacity to destroy all boundaries to release the limbs, heart, and soul to freedom.[50] The strength of love is violent, love's goal heroic—the privileged isle to which the poet hopes to woo the recovered Emily has a soul "like a buried lamp" that burns in the heart of the land.[51] This language of light culminates in the poet's vision of intermingling love:

> We shall become the same, we shall be one
> Spirit within two frames, oh! wherefore two?
> One passion in twin-hearts, which grows and grew,
> Till like two meteors of expanding flame,
> Those spheres instinct with it become the same,
> Touch, mingle, are transfigured; ever still
> Burning, yet ever inconsumable:
> . . . .
> Two overshadowing minds, one life, one death,
> One Heaven, one Hell, one immortality,
> And one annihilation.[52]

The "spheres instinct," fusing meteors, are the climax of Shelley's visions of interpenetrative, absorbing, life-giving sources of light. Such visions of heaven provoke, however, thoughts of hell, for the promise of immortality assures the mutuality of death. Shelley's triumphant hope of mutuality is dashed by his own words which cannot release themselves from their innate antithesis. Because his words do not have the strength to soar to the height of his vision, he lacks the power of his beloved, who, from her height, would pierce his heart.

Shelley's active, coalescing astronomy recalls Dickinson's even more anxious cosmology; however, hers is informed

---

[50] Ibid., 399-401.   [51] Ibid., 477.
[52] Ibid., 573-587.

by a fear of fusion, a desire for deferred union. Love, the power of life, and the central experience of death are all cast in terms of celestial phenomena—of light, fire, and the sun.

> The Admirations—and Contempts—of time—
> Show justest—through an Open Tomb—
> The Dying—as it were a Hight
> Reorganizes Estimate
> And what We saw not
> We distinguish clear—
> And mostly—see not
> What We saw before—
>
> 'Tis Compound Vision—
> Light—enabling Light—
> The Finite—furnished
> With the Infinite—
> Convex and Concave Witness—
> Back—toward Time—
> And forward—
> Toward the God of Him—   (906)

Whatever the specific genesis of the poem just quoted, here Dickinson takes as her subject the change in perspective, the shift in point of view, that follows death. The vision is "compound," life's opposite providing a new light by which to view the finite as the soul stares, Janus-like, back and forward through time. This terminal experience rather than love of an ideal form gives Dickinson the new light which shines around her. When she indulges in thoughts of the possibility of heaven, she imagines it in images of sight:

> In thy long Paradise of Light
> No moment will there be
> When I shall long for Earthly Play
> And mortal Company—   (1145)

Word and World

She does, however, describe the approach of life in terms of a fusion of fire, an intermingling of sparks reminiscent of Shelley's smouldering images:

> We met as Sparks—Diverging Flints
> Sent various—scattered ways—
> We parted as the Central Flint
> Were cloven with an Adze—
> Subsisting on the Light We bore
> Before We felt the Dark—
> We knew by change between itself
> And that etherial Spark. (958)

Unlike Shelley's vision of merging meteors, Dickinson sees the meeting as transitory, although it defines a new "angle of vision." They met, at random, thrust out from a diverging source; they part out of unity, split through by an adze to subsist on their memory of the lost light they had together created. Darkness can be identified only through its antithesis, former mutual light. The method of recounting this meeting and the departure depends on identifying each stage with its origins, as the initial union is characterized by each spark's flight *away* from a source. The history of their separation is defined by the central flint from which they are divided. Thus their new darkness inverts the earlier sanctified condition of light.

Dickinson's images of vision are often tied, as in Shelley's poems, to astronomical facts—the pattern of one form penetrating and dissolving into another. Yet characteristically, Dickinson questions this desire for such a merger, asserting instead the importance of an identity whose pattern allows no intrusion and whose shape suits it alone:

> The pattern of the sun
> Can fit but him alone
> For sheen must have a Disk
> To be a sun— (1550)

Word and World

The poem insists upon a distinct form to enable the quality, "sheen," to achieve its identity as sun, but interdependence may yet occur between the identities of sky and earth. Dickinson may, for instance, imagine herself as the sea which, *contra naturam*, controls the moon as the moon regulates the tides on earth. Celestial interdependence does not lead to the absorption of one body into another but suggests instead a reciprocity of power, a comingling of strength that creates mutual domination.

> I make His Crescent fill or lack—
> His Nature is at Full
> Or Quarter—as I signify—
> His Tides—do I control—
>
> He holds superior in the Sky
> Or gropes, at my Command
> Behind inferior Clouds—or round
> A Mist's slow Colonnade—
>
> But since We hold a Mutual Disc—
> And front a Mutual Day—
> Which is the Despot, neither knows—
> Nor Whose—the Tyranny— (909)

Dickinson imagines the waxing and waning of the moon as tides controlled by the "I" of the poem. This inversion recalls the moon vulnerable to the storm of the questor's sleep in *Epipsychidion*:

> What storms then shook the ocean of my sleep,
> Blotting that Moon, whose pale and waning lips
> Then shrank as in the sickness of eclipse;—
> And how my soul was as a lampless sea,
> And who was then its Tempest; and when She,
> The Planet of that hour, was quenched, what frost
> Crept o'er those waters, till from coast to coast
> The moving billows of my being fell
> Into a death of ice, immovable;—[53]

[53] *Ibid.*, 308-316.

Word and World

His storms blot or obstruct the vision of the moon that wanes as if in sickness; when the light of the moon is quenched, extinguished by the waters of his soul's storm, no light penetrates from her and his being sinks into the "death of ice." The relation of moon to sea becomes one of mutual control, for power rests in sea and moon to destroy or revive the other.

But Dickinson uses astronomical imagery most powerfully when she assigns a cosmic identity to the self, describing her existence as a voyage surrounded by the abstract realities of time. Alone and in danger, the self discovers no one present but her own perception:[54]

> Behind Me—dips Eternity—
> Before Me—Immortality—
> Myself—the Term between—
> Death but the Drift of Eastern Gray,
> Dissolving into Dawn away,
> Before the West begin—
>
> 'Tis Kingdoms—afterward—they say—
> In perfect—pauseless Monarchy—
> Whose Prince—is Son of None—
> Himself—His Dateless Dynasty—
> Himself—Himself diversify—
> In Duplicate divine—
>
> 'Tis Miracle before Me—then—
> 'Tis Miracle behind—between—
> A Crescent in the Sea—
> With Midnight to the North of Her—
> And Midnight to the South of Her—
> And Maelstrom—in the Sky— (721)

The form of these lines and the vision of the self surrounded by time, the waiting, open sea, and the prospect of a possi-

---

[54] For another interpretation of this poem see Charles R. Anderson's *Emily Dickinson's Poetry: Stairway of Surprise*, pp. 280-281.

ble, future kingdom closely resemble this moment in Shelley's "The Triumph of Life":

> . . . ; before me fled
> The night; behind me rose the day; the deep
> Was at my feet, and Heaven above my head,—[55]

Here Dickinson uses the Shelleyan structure of prepositions ("before" and "behind") in her first stanza but reverses their order. In Shelley's poem, the "I" sees himself carrying the dawn with him, culmination of the opening of the poem which describes the sunrise waking the earth. The poet awakens from a sleepless night of contemplation, and, as he rises with the dawn, a vision rolls upon the passive self engendering a trance, the waking dream of the poem. In Dickinson's opening stanza, there is also a dawn, but she is not a part of it. Death enters the cyclic process of life and dissolves into the East. Throughout this process, she remains a space or "term" between eternity and immortality. The second stanza presents a version of what others, those of the party of belief, have said exists in the world beyond. Rejecting this hearsay, Dickinson redefines her place by stripping it of the received terms of Eternity and Immortality, of death fading into the Dawn of a Heaven she knows at best will be miraculous—unaccounted for, and besides, not really expected. She stands

> With Midnight to the North of Her—
> And Midnight to the South of Her—
> And Maelstrom—in the Sky—

Perspective changes as the east-west association of the sun gives way to north-south—the polar appraisal of her condition. What Dickinson sees is not the dawn of the self as Shelley describes it in "The Triumph of Life," but a storm overhead, a naturalistic vision that replaces the religious language

[55] Shelley, "The Triumph of Life," 26-28.

Word and World

of her first two stanzas. Refusing the Orthodox consolations of the second strophe, she views the result—a self voyaging on the sea in darkness threatened by the tempest raging about her. But, after all, the possibility of accepting a palliative orthodoxy had vanished long ago. In a letter to the man she called her preceptor, T. W. Higginson, Dickinson writes: "They are religious—except me—and address an Eclipse, every morning—whom they call their 'Father.' "[56] In a similar image, Shelley, a fellow antinomian, identifies Christianity's failing after Christ:

> And Gregory and John; and men divine
>
> Who rose like shadows between man and God;
> Till that eclipse, still hanging over heaven,
> Was worshipped by the world o'er which they
> strode, . . .[57]

ASTRONOMICAL ABSORPTION for both poets is as much a threat as it is possible redemption, for both desire a unity between word and thing that in this life cannot be fulfilled, but instead either results in the irreconcilable difference between word and world or threatens a usurpation of the imagination as it is absorbed by the world. Whatever the possibilities for failure, however, Shelley and Dickinson manifest a Promethean courage. I want, therefore, to draw this discussion to a close by briefly examining Dickinson's response to the Promethean impulses in Shelley's verse. In a poem possibly written as a response to the mythic Prometheus, and perhaps with Shelley's *Prometheus Unbound* in mind, Dickinson writes:

> The smouldering embers blush—
> Oh Cheek within the Coal
> Hast thou survived so many nights?
> The smouldering embers smile—
> Soft stirs the news of Light

[56] Dickinson, letter no. 261, II, 404, April 1863.
[57] Shelley, "The Triumph of Life," 288-291.

Word and World

> The stolid Rafters glow
> One requisite has Fire that lasts
> Prometheus never knew— (1132)

This penciled worksheet draft suggests an alternative ending for the poem—"This requisite has Fire that lasts / It must at first be true—." Whether this change would have been adopted in a final draft we cannot know; however, it does indicate what, according to Dickinson as revisionist, Prometheus did not know—that the requisite condition for a lasting flame is faith.[58] Exactly why Prometheus should lack this faith, he who remains true to men but protests blind trust in Jupiter, remains a question. Yet, taken by itself, this poem asserts that what keeps the fire alive are the smouldering embers, feminine in their blushes, which feed the fires of love. When read in the context of the passage which may be its source, Dickinson's poem becomes more complex:

> Like veiled lightning asleep,
> Like the spark nursed in embers,
> The last look Love remembers,
> Like a diamond, which shines
> On the dark wealth of mines,
> A spell is treasured but for thee alone.
>   Down, down![59]

The Song of the Spirits in *Prometheus Unbound* leads Asia and Panthea to the Cave of Demogorgon, the form of the imageless deep, and ushers in their descent to the mystery of things.[60] The spell, preserved for them alone, reveals a Spirit which tells Asia and Panthea that God made and rules the world—the assertion of faith Prometheus will not accept. But the ultimate answer to why the world is as it has become

---

[58] See Johnson's note, *Poems*, II, p. 794.
[59] Shelley, *Prometheus Unbound*, II, iii, "Song of the Spirits," 83-89.
[60] Pulos comments on the possibility of reaching the core of things: "Reality for Shelley, as for Hume, would have to remain an unknown quantity—called in *The Triumph of Life* (1. 396) 'the realm without a name' " (p. 52).

Word and World

remains a secret, for "the deep truth is imageless." Because Dickinson's lines appear alone, her poem does away with the context of a descent into the root of things. However, the smouldering embers, news of light illuminating the stolid rafters, and singular use of Prometheus' name, draw her poem into the "Song of the Spirits," with Dickinson's poem focusing on the embarrassed embers which have kept the flame alive. This constancy that has fed the flame is what Prometheus, he who delivers it and then departs, cannot know. Thus Dickinson may take a lyric fragment from a larger dramatic structure and transfer her emphasis to the faithful beloved as she simultaneously rebukes a doubting Prometheus, hero of the drama that serves as her source. Characteristically she removes all the *dramatis personae* except the self and one other—a gesture she makes whenever she incorporates lines into her own poems, replacing another's plot with her own priorities.

Another side of Dickinson's dark Prometheanism is her insistence upon an enabling sacrifice, the awareness of the need to inflict injury upon the self to release poetic power. In the following poem, Dickinson takes the horror of the eagle's eating Prometheus' liver and turns it into a self-reflexive gesture, a suicidal piercing of the soul:

> Sang from the Heart, Sire,
> Dipped my Beak in it,
> If the Tune drip too much
> Have a tint too Red
>
> Pardon the Cochineal—
> Suffer the Vermillion—
> Death is the Wealth
> Of the Poorest Bird.
>
> Bear with the Ballad—
> Awkward—faltering—
> Death twists the strings—
> 'Twas'nt my blame—

Word and World

> Pause in your Liturgies—
> Wait your Chorals—
> While I repeat your
> Hallowed name— (1059)

The poet becomes the bird who plucks the scarlet blood from her own heart to sing ballads for her "Sire"; she destroys the sinews of the self so that she speaks directly from her heart. Who is this Sire, and why must the poet sing a song requiring her death? Despite the penultimate "hallowed," we know that he is not God because he is conducting public rituals of worship, singing songs in praise of Divinity. She asks him to pause in his own prayer so that he may heed her voice. Interestingly, a suggested substitute for the "repeat" in line fifteen is "recite"—Dickinson may have rejected the substitution because it drew too much attention to her real subject, for the poem is about the poet herself singing from the heart, who finds there the name she wishes to praise. She repeats this name, and his identity fuses with her song. Yet the song is so much her own, its origin her life-blood, that there can be no question of its authenticity. She pleads for patience if her song displease her Sire; excess of emotion, the scarlet tinge, is due to the depth of her self-inflicted wound, a result of her desire to sing with complete honesty. She asks her religious sovereign to "pardon," to "suffer," the quality of her song—words which call for Christlike forgiveness and compassion. In an earlier poem, during a dialogue with Jesus in which she voices her own inadequacy, Dickinson protests, "I am spotted," and Jesus replies, "I am Pardon."[61] But, despite such religious identification, here the Sire himself remains an imitator of Christ, a Christian worshipper. The reasons for her halting ballad are imposed by death, which "twists the strings" of her lute, the instrument of the lyric she sings. At this moment, Dickinson becomes a poet who will sacrifice her own life in order

---

[61] Dickinson, Poem 964.

Word and World

to remain true, to sing for another who must be begged to hear her voice.

This self-destructive, sacrificial Promethean vision of the poet resembles Shelley's voice in "Ode to the West Wind" when he calls upon the natural strength of the vanquishing wind to carry his own words, the leaves falling from the dead "wood of suicide."[62] Just as Dickinson calls upon her Sire to heed her cry, he pleads with the voice of the wind to listen and cries, "oh, hear!" striving with the wind in his "sore need." Weightless he is rendered the wind's victim, borne up by it and as effortlessly dashed down: "I fall upon the thorns of life! I bleed!"[63] He pleads that he may become the lyre, passive yet essential to articulate the voice of the wind; yet his dead thoughts must be driven.[64] The only possibility which rises from such self-destruction is the power of an external, natural force—the wind itself. He commands it to act and to respond to his cry:

> Scatter, as from an unextinguished hearth
> Ashes and sparks, my words among mankind![65]

These ashes come from the burning soul of the poet; his plea is a final, desperate cry of hope. To the extent that Shelley and Dickinson see within the poetic act the necessity for self-destruction, Dickinson's vision of the self as a dying bird resembles Shelley's suicidal vision. Each must rely on the will of another—Dickinson's human, Shelley's natural. Whereas his aim is one of cosmic ambition, for he wishes the wind to carry his smouldering words through the world, Dickinson asks only for a moment's pause so that she can reach the single ear, her sole audience. Despite the differing

---

[62] These leaves falling from the dead "wood of suicide" recall those other leaves from Dickinson's poem which "unhooked themselves from Trees—" (Poem 824).
[63] Shelley, "Ode to the West Wind," 54.
[64] See "Ode to the West Wind," 63.
[65] *Ibid.*, 66-67.

identities and purpose of their songs, the necessity for self-immolation remains. Shelley and Dickinson reveal a shared perception of the origins of their art, the destruction within the act of the self making poems. Yet these poems illustrate the more fundamental divergence between them, for as Dickinson turns to the "other," who, in one of his guises represents a projection of the self, Shelley turns again for salvation to nature. And this difference points to a more general divergence. If Shelley's world mirrors to serve his apocalyptic vision, Dickinson internalizes the forces that surround her, assuming their cosmic rage and power. Isolating images from their intended poetic structure, she places them within her own context, identifying the self as an antetype, the origin for all naturalistic metaphors. Enticed by those moments when Shelley weds the physical to the abstract, when arrows pierce the heart, hounds flee like hours, lightnings sound, Dickinson recognizes that each of these images contains within it the germ of a possible structure for a poem or metaphor, which, examined for its own dramatic potential, can then be identified and associated with the life of the self.

This discussion of imagistic connections between Shelley and Dickinson, as well as the textual analyses on which it depends, develops from my conviction that it is through such an approach that we may begin to learn about Dickinson's reading of Shelley and therefore about her own strategies of composition. At this chapter's close, I want finally to call to your attention a few specific verbal echoes of Shelley in Dickinson's work and briefly mention other aspects of similarity. Reading Dickinson one hears numerous instances of Shelleyan diction which might be traced to specific sources. One reads Poem 1137, "The duties of the Wind are few," and thinks of its relationship to "Ode to the West Wind." In *Prometheus Unbound*, I, i, 477, Shelley writes "Prometheus, Pain is my element, as hate is thine; / Ye rend me now: I care not," and Dickinson: "Pain—has an Element of Blank—"(Poem 650). Or consider the possible links between Poem 1694:

Word and World

> The wind drew off
> Like hungry dogs
> Defeated of a bone
> Through fissures in
> Volcanic cloud
> The yellow lightning shone—
> The trees held up
> Their mangled limbs
> Like animals in pain
> When Nature falls upon herself
> Beware an Austrian

and the "Lines written among the Euganean Hills": "And the eastern Alpine snow, / Under the mighty Austrian." The symbol of political repression fuses in Shelley's poem with the disruption of nature. Perhaps recalling this fusion, Dickinson could be suggesting that one should heed the signs of nature which presage the stranger, the "Austrian" of Shelley's poem. Or, to cite one final instance of possible verbal echo, Dickinson's "Wild Nights—Wild Nights!" (Poem 249) surely bears more than an external relation to "Good-night," also a poem about remaining together, staying close or voyaging from the beloved. The importance of these echoes lies in their suggestiveness; one way or another, Shelley's voice seems to have entered Dickinson's poems. Another more important kinship, however, lies in Shelley's and Dickinson's conceptions of the privileged moment, the inspiriting occasion. For both poets, the artist is visited by another power; he is visited by the word.[66] (See Dickinson's Poem 1452, "Your thoughts dont have words everyday.")

---

[66] For a discussion of passivity and inspiration, see Harold Bloom, *Shelley's Mythmaking* (Ithaca: Cornell University Press, 1969), p. 37. Later in the book, Bloom speaks of Shelley's "morning and evening star symbolism by which Shelley pictures poetry itself as vanishing relationship . . ." (p. 218). It is in departing and fading that Dickinson also claims she is most at her ease. Departure becomes a source of value and comfort: "To disappear enhances— / The Man that runs away / Is tinctured for an instant / With Immortality" (Poem 1209). (See also Poem 1349.)

Word and World

Just how Dickinson excises images from their origins both in other poets and in the natural world tells us most about what she values and how she conceives of the act of writing poems. If Shelley's world is a mirror, reflecting his apocalyptic vision, Dickinson fuses the identity, as the thing itself becomes something else. Because Dickinson uses the language of the natural to describe a process which she hopes may allow her to pass beyond the limits of cyclic nature, her images serve an alternative purpose which parallels but must differ essentially from their natural origins. Whereas Shelley calls upon the strength of a sublime and startling nature to serve his own poetic vision of a turbulent, responsive world that provokes and reflects internal mental experience, Dickinson severs lightning, thunder, and wind from their natural contexts to reassign them the mythic value of types representing the recurrent, internal events that inform her life. Such an internal and private identification of natural images signifies not a surrender to the natural but a more complete usurpation of it, as the reflexive identity of these images works toward achieving a radical independence for the solipsistic imagination.

V

Emerson, Dickinson, and the Abyss

> He who fights with monsters should be careful lest he thereby become a monster. And if thou gaze long into an abyss, the abyss will also gaze into thee. —Friedrich Nietzsche

ARACHNE, maiden of legendary audacity, claimed she could weave more splendidly than the goddess Minerva herself; the challenge ended in self-inflicted death and metamorphosis into a spider—the cunning revenge of the Divine weaver. Dickinson betrays a similar boldness, placing her poems against the most powerful voices for her generation—the poets of Romanticism. Like the Romantics, she writes quest poems, for they seek to complete the voyage, to prove the strength of the imagination against the stubbornness of life, the repression of an antithetical nature, and that "hidden mystery," the final territory of death. The form of the poems reflects their subject. She writes poems of "radical inquiry,"[1] riddles that tease the intelligence or alternatively achieve startling definitions which testify to the authority of her own consciousness. Such authority depends on power, and it is power that lies at the center of Dickinson's relation to Emerson. It is from Emerson that she learns the terms of the struggle and what she needs to conquer—to write poems that win from nature the triumph of freedom for the imagination.

Each of us holds a particular, if hidden, resentment to-

---

[1] Glauco Cambon writes, "A significant poem by Emily Dickinson often takes shape as an act of radical inquiry." "Emily Dickinson and the Crisis of Self-Reliance" (*Transcendentalism and Its Legacy*, ed. Myron Simon and Thornton H. Parsons, Ann Arbor: University of Michigan Press, 1969), p. 125.

wards the voice that first liberates us. How strong the antagonistic joy for Dickinson to read, almost in "credo" form, a validation of her initial aims in Emerson's essay, "The Poet"! The controlling image of poet as reader of the universe leads to his observing minute particulars, studying his relation to the text, his subject-symbol, finding what will suffice as an adequate symbol for the self. The poet must be more than a scrupulous reader, for "there is no fact in nature which does not carry the whole sense of nature," and even he is part of the process itself: "We are symbols and inhabit symbols." To carry the creative emphasis further, the "poet is the Namer or Language-maker."[2] In conclusion, all is in nature, and the force of the poet's imagination determines his success in hearing and reading the natural world. Emerson had yet to learn, in 1842, what he knew later—that such certain knowledge, a complete ability to read a text, was beyond any human poet. In "Experience," Emerson was to envision both life and the man living it as the result of illusions. The individual is limited to creating the illusion determined by his own qualities; we are left with the power to live within our self-created deceptions: "Dream delivers us to dream, and there is no end to illusion. . . . We animate what we can, and we see only what we animate. Nature and books belong to the eyes that see them."[3] And, a little later in the essay, Emerson emphasizes the negative aspects of this personal dream: "Temperament also enters fully into the system of illusions and shuts us in a prison of glass which we cannot see."[4]

In response to the Emerson of "The Poet," Dickinson works out her own solution as she asserts that nature is not the sacred text, ready to reveal all if we read it right. She contends not only that we can never attain to full knowledge

---

[2] Ralph Waldo Emerson, "The Poet," *Selections from Ralph Waldo Emerson: An Organic Anthology*, ed. Stephen E. Whicher (Boston: Houghton, Mifflin Company, 1960), pp. 229-231.

[3] Emerson, "Experience," *Essays: Second Series* (Boston and New York: Houghton, Mifflin and Company, 1876), p. 50.

[4] *Ibid.*, pp. 51-52.

The Abyss

of nature, that our view is dominated by our eye; she extends the negative cast of Emerson's opening pages of "Illusions": "There is illusion that shall deceive even the elect. There is illusion that shall deceive even the performer of the miracle. Though he make his body, he denies it."[5] For her, nature becomes an antagonist, a deeply equivocal mystery, certainly exquisite at times, but with an exotic power that withholds its secrets as it dazzles. No matter how well one reads or imagines, nature as text withdraws and guards its final lesson; morality departs from the natural world to depend solely upon the individual. Consequently, the self perceives nature as an adversary and seeks to go beyond it into an anti- or post-naturalistic environment, pursuing questions in a self-dominated sphere that rejects the province of a communal, natural life. Finally, nature becomes not a sacred ground but a place that fails to protect, from which she must withdraw to ask other kinds of questions. Dickinson cannot accept the uneasy position Emerson maintains at the close of "Illusions": "If life seem a succession of dreams, yet poetic justice is done in dreams also." Nor can she subscribe to the conclusion to "Experience": a reiteration of justice and the rather belated assurance that "the true romance which the world exists to realize will be the transformation of genius into practical power."[6] Abandonment of the problem fails to satisfy; nor is she temperamentally able to achieve the solace Emerson rises to attain: "For we transcend the circumstances continually and taste the real quality of existence. . . . We see God face to face every hour, and know the savor of Nature."[7] Such compromises appear evasions to Dickinson, and she turns from them to seek her own accommodation to the dilemma Emerson described in his "Ode to Beauty":

> I dare not die
> In Being's deeps past ear and eye;

[5] Emerson, "Illusions," *The Conduct of Life* (Boston and New York: Houghton, Mifflin and Company, 1960), pp. 319-320.

[6] Emerson, "Experience," *Essays: Second Series*, p. 86.

[7] Emerson, "Illusions," *The Conduct of Life*, pp. 323-324.

The Abyss

> Lest there I find the same deceiver
> And be the sport of Fate forever.
> Dread Power, but dear! if God thou be,
> Unmake me quite, or give thyself to me!⁸

If nature is no longer at the center and cannot hold the answers she seeks, what of vision, the significance of sight? What becomes of the crucial Emersonian "eye" if the "text" cannot be read anyway? Although vision remains a major concern, she antithetically praises what she cannot see, either because the moment is past, distant, or denied. She defines through negation the positive values Emerson had praised in "Nature," "Circles," and "The Poet." She cannot believe that "a flash of his eye burns up the veil";⁹ and the pattern of this failure, its procedures and disappointments, assumes priority for her imagination.

> Sweet Skepticism of the Heart—
> That knows—and does not know—
> And tosses like a Fleet of Balm—
> Affronted by the snow—
> Invites and then retards the Truth
> Lest Certainty be sere
> Compared with the delicious throe
> Of transport thrilled with Fear—¹⁰ (1413)

Internal qualities developed in response to an impenetrable natural world determine her strength and inform her character; she chooses to fly "with Pinions of Disdain."¹¹

---

⁸ Emerson, "Ode to Beauty," *Poems* (Boston and New York: Houghton, Mifflin and Company, 1904), p. 311.

⁹ Emerson, "Circles," *Essays: First Series* (Boston and New York: Houghton, Mifflin and Company, 1865), p. 311.

¹⁰ Evan Carton, in his recent essay, "Dickinson and the Divine: The Terror of Integration, The Terror of Detachment" (*ESQ: A Journal of the American Renaissance*, 25:242-252), argues that "images of blindness or thwarted vision . . . usually signify achievement or its potential, rather than frustration" (p. 243).

¹¹ Dickinson, Poem 1431, line 1, Vol. III, p. 992.

The Abyss

If Dickinson turns from the nature espoused by the early Emerson, denying its moral imperative, she also simultaneously relinquishes his doctrines of compensation and correspondence. No justice can be expected, no resemblance between self and the landscape maintained, once morality disappears from the universe of things. Emerson, at the age of twenty and writing for himself, stated most strongly what was to be an essential element for his own philosophical position: his ability to rise above circumstance into moments of ecstatic fulfillment. "Rend away the darkness," he writes, "and restore to man the knowledge of this principle [a moral universe], and you have lit the sun over the world and solved the riddle of life."[12] Dickinson abjures this possibility, for when she surveys the landscape for evidence of the moral imperative she finds it lacking. Instead, Dickinson learns that nature is often capricious, disinterested, or cruel. By rejecting a moral nature, she cuts herself off from the comforts of a compensatory philosophy and a benevolent view of life which allows Emerson the privilege, when he can reach it, of escaping the ground of discouraging circumstance.

Dickinson, however, does seek correspondence between herself and nature, but her own consciousness must dictate the relationship; the landscape becomes an allegorical projection of her internal drama as her poems present a spectrum of reaction to the amorality of nature—from hope and exultation to despair. If nature cannot be relied upon as a way to approach the spiritual world and lead us from Secondary to Primary Causes, she must go by another route, approach immortality not through nature but in a direct confrontation with death. The poems' most ambitious attempt is, therefore, to provide us, the living, with the experience of hearing a voice speaking from the dead. They anticipate, observe, and follow the movements of the dying. This concentration on final moments is Dickinson's protest against the inviolate silence of death. What she wants, what "is best," the poems

[12] This Journal passage is quoted by Sherman Paul in *Emerson's Angle of Vision: Man and Nature in American Experience* (Cambridge: Harvard University Press, 1952), p. 90 (J.I. 257ff.)

The Abyss

tell us, lies beyond her power, in realms of impossibility. It is past life that Dickinson wishes to draw her circle. If consciousness bestows power, she must carry her awareness beyond the grave, invading the forbidden territory with her voice. Emerson had asserted the potency of the energizing spirit to break through all boundaries, to rise above circumstance. Dickinson, with a daring literalism, attempts to face her central antagonist directly, to draw a circle around the fact of death. Emerson preaches the strength of the individual: "But if the soul is quick and strong it bursts over that boundary on all sides and expands another orbit on the great deep, which also runs up into a high wave, with attempt again to stop and to bind. But the heart refuses to be imprisoned; in its first and narrowest pulses it already tends outward with a vast force and to immense and innumerable expansions."[13]

Dickinson's poems face the barrier of mortality and confront Emerson's challenge: "There is no outside, no inclosing wall, no circumference to us. . . . His only redress is forthwith to draw a circle outside of his antagonist."[14] He perceives this power during isolated moments; the freedom of that moment from the past determines its potential for imaginative transformation: "In nature every moment is new; the past is always swallowed and forgotten; the coming only is sacred. Nothing is secure but life, transition, the energizing spirit."[15] Her poems strive not for the moment in nature that is new but a space beyond it which provides a retrospective vision on life—the freedom of evaluation after the event. During life, however, there are moments which potentially speak of the mysteries to be disclosed in death, and it is the poet's task to witness these occasions and discover their meaning:

> . . . .
> The Moments of Dominion
> That happen on the Soul

[13] Emerson, "Circles," *Essays: First Series,* p. 304.
[14] *Loc.cit.*
[15] Emerson, "Circles," pp. 319-320.

The Abyss

> And leave it with a Discontent
> Too exquisite—to tell—
> . . . . (627)

The secret of the landscape will reveal itself only after life departs, when the taunts of an unknowable nature cease. Until then, "The Pleading of the Summer—" and "That other Prank—of Snow—" will not disclose their secret:

> . . . .
> Their Graspless manners—mock us—
> Until the Cheated Eye
> Shuts arrogantly—in the Grave—
> Another way—to see— (627)

Only the thinnest of veils, life, prevents her from winning this necessary vision. Another poem, in the same packet, and most probably written in the same year, 1862, asserts Dickinson's frustration in Divine, mercantile terms which combine the bitterness of defeat with an attack on the doctrine of compensation itself:

> I asked no other thing—
> No other—was denied—
> I offered Being—for it—
> The Mighty Merchant sneered—
>
> Brazil? He twirled a Button—
> Without a glance my way—
> 'But—Madam—is there nothing else—
> That We can show—Today?' (621)

She finds other subjects, but Brazil—the ultimate exotic— remains an adequate symbol for the unifying quest of her poems. The challenge she faces is the inability to speak clearly from the other side of the grave. Deploring the inevitable silence, Dickinson will write poems that go so far as to deny death's inevitability and hover on the threshold between life and death. Prolepsis becomes a crucial strategy because it allows her to supersede the strictures of life. More-

The Abyss

over, passion extends to others' final moments as well; for, it is through death that the mutual condition of solipsism is simultaneously consolidated and dissolved.

Loss of belief, of a Christian or even an Emersonian faith, points toward the origins of her grim obsession:

> Those—dying then,
> Knew where they went—
> They went to God's Right Hand—
> That Hand is amputated now
> And God cannot be found—
>
> The abdication of Belief
> Makes the Behavior small—
> Better an ignis fatuus
> Than no illume at all— (1551)

Nullifying the integrity of the flame as the poem names it denies the possibility of belief. Always haunted by the forbidden, Dickinson merges memories of childhood lures, the "Flower Hesperian," with the promise of the dead. A worksheet draft written late in the poet's life specifies this preeminent concern with the moment of another's death:

> Still own thee—still thou art
> What surgeons call alive—
> Though slipping—slipping I perceive
> To thy reportless Grave—
>
> Which question shall I clutch—
> What answer wrest from thee
> Before thou dost exude away
> In the recallless sea? (1633)

The poem wants answers and is willing to clutch the question, to wrestle with the dying, for response. No other thing is denied, and the intensity of inquiry stems not from a life of despair but from an increasingly complete hegemony of consciousness that is deprived only of what it most craves to

The Abyss

make it complete. Such extremity accounts, in large measure, for the polarities of the poems—the radically fluctuating moods that confront us as we read.

No forward or backward can be measured when the goal remains inviolate. Acknowledging that "no man saw awe," Dickinson asserts that we cannot come back bearing the vision, for "returning is a different route, The spirit could not show." Dickinson describes this geography of impossibility, a terrain one needs to cross before the journey begins: "Three Rivers and a Hill to cross / One Desert and a Sea."[16] At the moment of completion, the fulfillment of her quest, mortality intercedes. With customary boldness, she names Death itself as the agent of usurpation; he walks off with the prize rightfully her own. In the face of this defeat, Dickinson places her poems, literally experiments that presume against the possible. She writes, "Experiment escorts us last—" and beneath "escorts" she places, then crosses out, "accosts." The polarity of feeling, the inner dialectic of what her "experiments" mean to her, cannot be more adequately conveyed than by these two words and their "correction."[17]

Emerson challenges Dickinson to explore her power, but what saves him fails her needs. His darkest voice forms the background against which she composes poems. The opening to "Circles," an essay that deeply affected Dickinson, states the potency of expansion for the eye.

"The eye is the first circle; the horizon which it forms is the second; and throughout nature this primary figure is repeated without end. It is the highest emblem in the cipher of the world. St. Augustine described the nature of God as a circle whose centre was everywhere and its circumference nowhere. We are all our lifetime reading the copious sense of this first of forms. One moral we have already deduced in considering the circular or compensatory character of every human action. Another analogy we shall now trace, that every action admits of being outdone. Our life is an apprenticeship to the truth that around every circle another can be

---

[16] Dickinson, Poem 1664. [17] Dickinson, Poem 1770.

The Abyss

drawn; that there is no end in nature, but every end is a beginning; There is always another dawn risen on mid-noon, and under every deep a lower deep opens."[18]

The possibility of a "lower deep," a more potent mystery to conquer, becomes, for Dickinson, the abyss; expansion opens into emptiness. She cannot abide the thought of fathomless depths, for they offer not opportunity but the terror of imminent destruction, an utter dissolution of the self. Emerson's faith in our capacity to expand into such depths depends upon his effect as a teacher—his ability to awaken us from our lapse, our temporary degeneracy. Only in such a state of slipping degradation are we estranged from nature and God. "As we degenerate, the contrast between us and our house is more evident. We are as much strangers in nature as we are aliens from God."[19] He heralds the need for a liberating poet to restore us to an adequate awareness of our own possibilities. Through a series of comparisons between this sublime potential and our current condition, Emerson asserts the illimitable power lurking within: "Once man was all; now he is an appendage, a nuisance."[20] The fault can be remedied, if only we heed his call. And throughout all the later, more sober, modulations of his thought, the belief that

---

[18] Emerson, "Circles," *Essays: First Series*, p. 301. In this passage, Emerson himself incorporates Miltonic echoes (see *Paradise Lost*, V, 310f., IV, 76f., and X, 842-44), and by converting these to his own purposes, he asserts the shaping power of the eye. This process of composition—the simultaneous suppression of Miltonic quotations and the hidden appeal to their original contexts—provides an implicit commentary on the capacity of Emerson's own literary eye. Once recognized by the reader, the character of these allusions confirms that the human activity Emerson has in mind is that a literary imagination performs on a written text. The success of this double communication depends upon our recognition that Emerson is offering an example of re-forming material as he advocates this activity The reader must fulfill the authorial intention; consequently Emerson engages the reader in a reciprocal activity—he is invited to participate in the development of expanding "horizons" of meaning which depend not only on the author's but on the reader's mediating vision.

[19] Emerson, *Selections from Ralph Waldo Emerson: An Organic Anthology*, p. 50.

[20] Ibid., "The Divinity School Address," p. 104.

The Abyss

"intellect annuls Fate. So far as a man thinks, he is free," remains firm.[21] In his early proclamation, "Nature," Emerson states this essential center to his future meditations: "The ruin or the blank that we see when we look at nature, is in our own eye."[22] The material world remains subordinate to the power of the single mind, and, though he may sink into a temporary despair, or realize the necessity of accepting some principle of Fate, Emerson retains his belief in the power of the imagination to rise above despondency and conquer the conditions of life.

But there are moments in Emerson when despair takes over, and it is during these that he sounds most like Dickinson. In a journal entry marked "Skepticism," Emerson states, "There are many skepticisms. The universe is like an infinite series of planes, each of which is a false bottom, and when we think our feet are planted now at last on the adamant, the slide is drawn out from under us."[23] Over twenty years later, he expresses the relation of the Me and the Not-Me when the false bottom slips: "There may be two or three or four steps, according to the genius of each, but for every seeing soul there are two absorbing facts,—*I and the Abyss.*"[24] This comes closest to Dickinson's vision of the problem she confronts. Here is a struggle to know, to dive into the abyss and extract from it the knowledge she cannot win from nature or any other mediate experience. She agrees with Emerson when he remarks: "I am very content with knowing, if only I could know. That is an august entertainment, and would suffice me a great while."[25] But the salves Emerson applies to heal the wound between "I and the abyss" remain temperamentally unavailable to Dickinson. She cannot rely on a central self, a single, inner core. When she turns to it, she finds a consciousness that hides when she approaches, an inner adversary as threatening as any she faces from outside.

[21] *Ibid.,* "Fate," p. 340.
[22] *Ibid.,* "Nature," p. 55.
[23] *Ibid.,* p. 281, Autumn, 1845.
[24] *Ibid.,* p. 405, September, 1866.
[25] *Ibid.,* "Experience," p. 273.

The Abyss

And so experience becomes for her, literally, a "going through peril," a walk along broken planks over the abyss of annihilation; a vertiginous threshold which offers only the terror of defeat.[26] Though the pit remains a threat to Emerson, he marshals against it the promise of the "over-seer," one who rises above, who stands erect, and climbs "the stairway of surprise"[27] to freedom. If "the world is nothing, the man is all," he will take advantage of his sovereignty.[28] "Let me ascend above my fate and work down upon my world."[29] The stance of the beholder yields him the safety he requires. To stand above and aside allows him the leisure to recollect experience. And in this act he imitates the Spirit beyond— "For it is only the finite that has wrought and suffered; the infinite lies stretched in smiling repose."[30] The eye of the observer is the gift of the poet and offers him imaginative freedom from the circumstances of life, the pain of existence. Such a perspective serves the world, for without man it would remain only "a remoter and inferior incarnation of God, a projection of God in the unconscious."[31] The human mind provides the consciousness that lends meaning to an otherwise un-self-conscious, hence powerless nature. Man is the vital, necessary force that unites God to his works. Moreover, if one goes deep enough into the self, he discovers this truth is applicable to all men; the Other for Emerson is the Self, whereas for Dickinson the self can and most often does become the demonic Other.[32]

---

[26] Glauco Cambon, in his "Emily Dickinson and the Crisis of Self-Reliance," *Transcendentalism and Its Legacy*, notes the meaning of "experience" for Dickinson. He writes, "In so doing, Miss Dickinson unwittingly revives the very origin of the word: *ex-perior*, 'to go through,' with the closely related *periculum*, 'peril,' and this determines the semantic structure of the whole poem."

[27] Emerson, "Merlin," in Whicher, p. 448.

[28] Emerson, "The American Scholar," in Whicher, p. 79.

[29] *Ibid.*, Journal entry for May 21, 1837, p. 63.

[30] *Ibid.*, Journal entry [February 16, 1837], p. 59.

[31] *Ibid.*, "Nature," p. 50.

[32] Glauco Cambon has suggested this distinction: "If for Emerson the Other was Self, an irresistible benevolence, for Miss Dickinson it was the self that could become a demonic Other." ("Emily Dickinson and the Crisis

The Abyss

The fluid conception of Self with its boundless potency allows Emerson to push past the border of confining limitations. In "Spiritual Laws," Emerson describes his concept of a self that asserts the requisite flexibility to enact his challenge: "A man is a method, a progressive arrangement; a selecting principle, gathering his like to him wherever he goes. He takes only his own out of the multiplicity that sweeps and circles round him. He is like one of those booms which are set out from the shore on rivers to catch driftwood, or like the loadstone amongst splinters of steel."[33] The self has a pattern, a set of tendencies, which attracts only complimentary forms to it. This fluid self becomes in Emerson's own career an evolving identity that alters its strategies but returns to address itself to fundamental questions.[34] Dickinson's transformation of this fluid self is among her more devastating achievements: from many selves, she names two, the self and the other. This "other" is consciousness, that awful internal stranger that she must repeatedly confront. Dickinson further polarizes the internal structure, for that other self is sexualized. He embodies the masculine, prepotent force that must be at once wooed and denied.

This choosing up sides and severely narrowing options determines the intensity of Dickinson's strongest poems. Lovers and friends feed the identities of self and other, but crucial action occurs within the single, split consciousness.

---

of Self-Reliance," p. 126). To this I would add that Emerson brings his sense of Self outward so that the deeper he goes within, the more he claims to discover about others. By incorporating the Other into the Self, Emerson can dissolve a distance he regards as threatening while preserving a space between himself and others which protects him from the potentially harsh presence of an antithetical reality. This, at least, appears to be his aim, although he often falls short of success. The split Dickinson discerns between Self and Other assumes an internalized existence within her mind. The Other—an adversarial spirit—inhabits one aspect of her split consciousness. This internal adversary is demonic because he possesses the power to destroy or bless the mind in which he resides.

[33] Emerson, "Spiritual Laws," *Essays: First Series*, p. 144.

[34] See James McIntosh's discussion of the Emersonian concept of self in *The Yale Review*, Vol. LXV, December 1975, pp. 232-240, "Emerson's Unmoored Self."

The Abyss

Such internal duality serves as a structure that governs her poems, demanding the exchange of worlds and encouraging an essentially dramatic form. This primal split in the self finds corollaries, most notably in an intense psychomachia—the struggle between the body and the soul. Self-division hardens into a basic austerity when the Emersonian multiplicity reduces to two. This process of consolidation, a toughening of position, points toward the central split between the poets themselves.

In his confrontation with Necessity, Emerson adopts specific strategies for survival. By summoning his ability to distance at least a part of the self, he is able to embrace an acquiescence that accepts the fact of a finally unknowable nature and an unalterable Fate. Saadi, the Emersonian fictive poet, maintains his cheerful equanimity because of his absence from immediate involvement; he sits a little to one side and concentrates on writing poems. The development of such an independent poet-figure is itself a part of Emerson's creation of the Observer within the self. As R. A. Yoder writes:

"The personality of the poet was a matter of long and serious concern which Emerson tried to resolve in poems, essays, and even in bits of fiction scattered through the journals. Much of the character of the emerging poet-figure is clearly autobiographical and an attempt to state his own concept of the poet's role. But gradually Emerson loosened the identification between himself and the character he created, so that in his later essays, as Whicher pointed out, there are a number of dramatic characters or alter egos who speak for different, often opposite, sets of ideas."[35]

By contrast, although Dickinson states that the "I" of her poems is not herself but "a supposed person," this separation exists outside the province of the text; it occurs before the formation of the "I" that speaks to us so directly from the heart of her poems.[36]

---

[35] R. A. Yoder, "Toward the 'Titmouse Dimension': The Development of Emerson's Poetic Style," *PMLA*, Vol. 87, March 1972, pp. 255-270.

[36] Dickinson, letter no. 268, II, 412, July 1862, to T. W. Higginson. Of

The Abyss

Emerson, however, rather than force solutions to what he perceives as a deepened division between the Me and the Not-Me, exploits this detachment which performs so incalculable a service: "What was food for remorse and regret on the plane of action, on the plane of intellection was matter for wonder. Even in his time of greatest enthusiasm some part of him had stood disengaged and aloof, and answered all interrogations, 'I, oh, I am only here to see.' "[37] Although in times of disillusion, the privilege of spectatorship assumes a more ominous cast and threatens numbness; the relief, stasis, and aesthetic distance offered by this power earn it a permanent role within the flux of Emersonian identity.

Alternative vision—the observing eye—becomes literalized and expanded in Whitman's version of the self that stands apart and above. But in Dickinson's poems the self assumes neither an Emersonian nor a Whitmanian form. Her observer is potentially a spy, for his sight is directed not toward nature, the Not-Me, but focuses inward, on the self from which he grew. He most often takes the shape of an adversary, another Consciousness that inhabits her mind and whose struggle Dickinson converts to poems. This other self may be best friend or deadly enemy—a love-hate relationship that assumes priority over any external commitment.

> The Soul unto itself
> Is an imperial friend—
> Or the most agonizing Spy—
> An Enemy—could send—
>
> Secure against it's own—
> No treason it can fear—

---

the three identities of the "I" the reader needs to recognize, two are sides of the divided self and the third is the voice of the poem, its speaker. This voice subsumes the obvious rhetorical ironies in the poems (for instance the adoption of the persona of a child). The very obviousness of this and similar rhetorical masks reduces the distance between the supposed "I" and the poet.

[37] Stephen E. Whicher, *Freedom and Fate: An Inner Life of Ralph Waldo Emerson* (Philadelphia: University of Pennsylvania Press, 1971), p. 132.

The Abyss

> Itself—it's Sovreign—of itself
> The Soul should stand in Awe— (683)

Despite this fundamental difference in their concepts of the Self, Emerson and Dickinson both find the origin of power within the individual. They assume a vocabulary normally ascribed to external, natural phenomena, and apply it to the inner life. Instances of this process of internalization recur throughout Emerson, and one does not have to look far to find him celebrating his own use of such language. Of man he declares: "But the lightning which explodes and fashions planets, maker of planets and suns, is in him."[38] And, in what was to become a favorite trope for Dickinson, Emerson elaborates further upon the power that resides within:

"The human mind cannot be enshrined in a person who shall set a barrier on any one side to this unbounded, unboundable empire. It is one central fire, which, flaming now out of the lips of Etna, lightens the capes of Sicily, and now out of the throat of Vesuvius, illuminates the towers and vineyards of Naples. It is one light which beams out of a thousand stars. It is one soul which animates all men."[39]

The lips of Etna and throat of Vesuvius, the oral and the volcanic, anticipate Dickinson's coupling of voice and flame. Threat of eruption, for both poets, emanates from the mouth:

> When Etna basks and purrs
> Naples is more afraid
> Than when she shows her Garnet Tooth—
> Security is loud— (1146)

Whereas Emerson and Dickinson are both drawn to the vision of an imminent power that smoulders undetected, Dickinson "personalizes" this vision. Volcanic force is no longer

---

[38] Emerson, "Fate," *The Conduct of Life* (Boston and New York: Houghton, Mifflin and Company, 1866), p. 22.

[39] Emerson, "The American Scholar," *Selections from Ralph Waldo Emerson*, ed. Whicher, p. 76.

The Abyss

associated with universal man as in "The American Scholar," but, instead, with the single life. Power does not run through all of us, as Emerson maintains; furthermore, it cannot be apprehended by anyone who observes the seemingly quiet, single self. The one soul which animates all men now stands isolated and alone.

> A still—Volcano—Life—
> That flickered in the night—
> When it was dark enough to do
> Without erasing sight—
>
> A quiet—Earthquake Style—
> Too subtle to suspect
> By natures this side Naples—
> The North cannot detect
>
> The Solemn—Torrid—Symbol—
> The lips that never lie—
> Whose hissing Corals part—and shut—
> And Cities—ooze away— (601)

This single life erupts irrevocably. Hidden, mysterious, still, the power floods mechanically; corals "part and shut"—destroying cities. What distinguishes this from Emerson's volcano is Dickinson's insistence on secrecy, on individuality, and on destruction. The poems will go further to identify this oral potency with both poetry and the self.

Moreover, Dickinson's practice of defining her self against Emerson's while drawing upon his language recurs in varying forms. Although she may alter the thrust of an Emersonian image or impose her own priorities on his diction, the new poem lies hidden in its parent text. Characteristically, a Dickinson poem takes an example that Emerson introduces into an essay and invests it with the strength of a subversive, anti-Emersonian vision. For instance, in his essay "Fate," Emerson develops a series of paragraphs that open with a general, declarative sentence followed by specific occasions which enumerate the forms his generalizations assume. One paragraph in this series supplants the "listing" of examples with an encapsulated narrative:

"The force with which we resist these torrents of tendency looks so ridiculously inadequate that it amounts to little more than a criticism or protest made by a minority of one, under compulsion of millions. I seemed in the height of a tempest to see men overboard struggling in the waves, and driven about here and there. They glanced intelligently at each other, but 'twas little they could do for one another; 'twas much if each could keep afloat alone. Well, they had a right to their eye-beams, and all the rest was Fate."[40]

Emerson's example comes at the close of a series that climaxes in his assertion of our utter helplessness against the facts of nature, the fatality of our gestures against the end: "We cannot trifle with this reality, this cropping-out in our planted gardens of the core of the world. No picture of life can have any veracity that does not admit the odious facts. A man's power is hooped in by a necessity which, by many experiments, he touches on every side until he learns its arc."[41] Emerson uses the drowning swimmers to enlist our sympathy while driving home the truth of the reality that affects us all. Dickinson's description of a related drowning is instructive.

> Two swimmers wrestled on the spar—
> Until the morning sun—
> When One—turned smiling to the land—
> Oh God! the Other One!
>
> The stray ships—passing—
> Spied a face—
> Upon the waters borne—
> With eyes in death—still begging raised—
> And hands—beseeching—thrown! (201)

---

[40] Emerson, "Fate," *The Conduct of Life*, p. 19.
[41] *Ibid.*, pp. 19-20.

The Abyss

One swimmer appears to *cause* the other's drowning, or, at least, offers him no help. He is clearly victorious, and at dawn returns triumphant toward shore. Dickinson shifts our attention to the "Other One," who is spied but ignored by the ships that pass as he sinks, still pleading, toward death. Emerson left his swimmers to Fate, choosing to emphasize that the glances exchanged by the drowning men could not save them, that indeed men are helpless to save even themselves in the presence of such a force; but Dickinson stresses the accountability of one swimmer for the other's death, as well as the prolonged moment of helplessness of the drowned. Ships that pass do not even attempt to help; they are "stray," random, without purpose, yet they do not pause; without so much as the excuse of destination, they abandon the pleading man to his death. The poem explodes the event, opening it to its own narrative emphases—wrestling, human responsibility, the concentration on the eyes in death. Paradoxically, this sharpening of focus magnifies the moment by an act of compression. Blame is localized; the point of view partial. With these shifts in emphasis, Dickinson renders impossible Emerson's acceptance of an impersonal, impenetrable Fate; agencies of solution—the power of the self, its relation to the Over-Soul, a capacity to grow erect—fail Dickinson. Her self is split, and nature remains a mystery immune to the power of even so masterful an intellect as her own. The mediating experience of nature deceives more than it satisfies. She defines existence as a series of descents into the abyss:

> Emerging from an Abyss and entering it again—that is Life, is it not?[42]

Dickinson's poems announce how it is to live on the edge of such danger. Fear of falling assumes precedence over the possibility of flight.

---

[42] Prose Fragment 32. See letter no. 1024, *The Letters of Emily Dickinson*, Vol. III, p. 916.

The Abyss

> A Pit—but Heaven over it—
> And Heaven beside, and Heaven abroad;
> And yet a Pit—
> With Heaven over it.
>
> To stir would be to slip—
> To look would be to drop—
> To dream—to sap the Prop
> That holds my chances up.
> Ah! Pit! With Heaven over it!
>
> The depth is all my thought—
> I dare not ask my feet—
> 'Twould start us where we sit
> So straight you'd scarce suspect
> It was a Pit—with fathoms under it
> Its Circuit just the same
> Seed—summer—tomb—
> Whose Doom to whom (1712)

The circuit of the pit (the path around it) is marked by the stages of life: the seed = birth, summer = maturity, and the tomb of death. The cycle of life itself walks on the edge, with no possibility of escape except a heaven that remains tantalizingly beside, abroad, and above it. The "I" is left with awe and the abyss, extremes that cause her to guard each step she takes as she rounds the circle.

> I stepped from Plank to Plank
> A slow and cautious way
> The Stars about my Head I felt
> About my Feet the Sea.
>
> I knew not but the next
> Would be my final inch—
> This gave me that precarious Gait
> Some call Experience. (875)

As the danger of her position increases, as her world is reduced to heaven and the abyss, to the stars and the sea, her

The Abyss

own figure enlarges to fill the gap. Self assumes the gigantic proportions of one who touches the extremities of the universe. The radical severity of her world demands a self that will fill "the Term between."[43] This giantism corresponds to the aims of the expanded self that desires to measure the abyss. Thus, her poems speak with the power of an enclosed solipsism, the voice of compression. By single moments alone can Dickinson chart her course into the heart of the abyss and map her way out of it. She warns both herself and us that "slipping—is Crashe's law"; the next moment may signal another descent.[44]

What both Emerson and Dickinson call the abyss finds at least one of its origins in Jonathan Edwards' blazing pit of Hell. The terror his description instilled in the hearts of the congregation echoes in his wayward disciples: "Unconverted men walk over the pit of hell on a rotten covering, and there are innumerable places in this covering so weak that they will not bear their weight, and these places are not seen."[45] The void of the unknown, the mystery of the abyss, has replaced the certainty of the flames of Hell, but the central image of our own thoughtless instability as we walk on rotten planks remains. By placing the supreme power within the individual, Emerson removed much of the fear of the emptiness beneath us, but Dickinson restores to the pit its rightful terror, not by an orthodox vision of Divine retribution, but with her own forbidding gift. She would have been moved by Edwards' vision of "the dreadful pit of the glowing flames of the wrath of God," substituting only her doubt for his certainty. Identical, however, is her tenuous position, the precariousness of the self: "You hang by a slender thread, with the flames of divine wrath flashing about it. . . ."[46] She recognizes this condition, except in her abyss the

---

[43] Dickinson, Poem 721.   [44] Dickinson, Poem 997.

[45] Jonathan Edwards, "Sinners in the Hands of an Angry God" (*Jonathan Edwards: Representative Selections*, ed. Clarence H. Faust and Thomas H. Johnson, New York: Hill and Wang, 1962), p. 159.

[46] *Ibid.*, p. 165. Although Edwards' use of the image of the pit is emblematic of the Calvinist vision of Hell that both Emerson and Dickinson would remember, they would certainly be aware of other abysses that open up

The Abyss

flames are self-generated, created by the power of her own imagination. Furthermore, hers is an abyss that she tells us she can enter, and so it must be an internal, deeper part of the mind to which she descends and from which she emerges through the act of writing poems.

The fact that Dickinson's abyss lies within, that it resides in her psyche, grows from Emerson's assertion that the mind contains limitless possibilities. Ironically, what Dickinson achieves by fusing the threat of the Edwardsean pit with the Emersonian faith in the self is a devastating subversion of Emersonian power. She couples the mind's power with the terrors of hell to create, in an act of daring perversion, an unfathomable creature of her own mind—a pit she must enter for her salvation but a pit that holds within it the capacity to destroy the creative self.

Dickinson, in this radical act, recalls the specter of Arachne, who claims her superiority, usurping the sovereignty of others to weave a taut web above a pit of her own making. If the points of Dickinson's web touch the bottom of the pit, they also stretch to the heaven above it. The poems alone prove the wisdom of her demonic maneuver, a power won through the subversive risk of Arachnean form.

---

before men both in America and elsewhere. Geoffrey Hartman writes: "the Abyssal Vision has a history going from well-known biblical sources (Genesis and Psalms) through Virgil, Boehme, Thomas Burnet and other metaphysician-travelers of the profound. It culminates, prior to Wordsworth, in one of the really exciting though still self-flagellating bursts of sublimity in Thomson's *Seasons*, as the poet addresses the Genius of Science and is rewarded by a short if powerful response: . . ." (Hartman then quotes the passage.) (Geoffrey H. Hartman, *Wordsworth's Poetry: 1787-1814* [New Haven and London: Yale University Press, 1967], p. 196.) See also note 91, pp. 387-388, for Hartman's list of secondary sources which allude to this tradition.

VI

Afterword: On the Origins of Difference

AS ONE READS Dickinson through and against Wordsworth, Keats, Shelley, and Emerson, the origins of her dissent take on new meaning. Although she shares with them a faith in the sovereignty of the imagination and a belief in its powers, her skepticism—a distrust of nature and insistence upon the primacy of the mind—extends and intensifies one side of a dialectic already shaping Romantic thought. In response to what Wordsworth, Keats, Shelley, and Emerson recognize as the potentially disintegrative danger of a poetics that relies too heavily upon the single imagination, each finds ways of acknowledging the world which offer solace and afford varying degrees of protection against the dangers of a too intense imaginative isolation.

Dickinson contends, however, that, no matter how beguiling or beautiful, nature cannot be trusted to answer her most persistent questions: why we live, why we suffer, why we die. No naturalizing Romanticism can satisfy her skeptical imagination. One by one she eschews the Romantics' compensatory gestures, not by banishing them from her poetry, but by modifying them to conform to her vision. At the heart of Dickinson's subversion of Romantic gestures toward consolation is a reassessment of the premise behind each gesture, a redefining of the dualism which governs the Romantic conception of the world and the imagination. By insisting upon the sovereignty of the single consciousness, she finds the only solace available lies in her creation of a separate reality based upon the divisive forces within this imperial self. Such internalization produces not a diminution but a reaffirmation of her doubts, as distrust turns inward. When individual consciousness becomes all, when the balance shifts from imagination and the world to the self alone, loss of consciousness or death becomes even more catastrophic than before. Yet it is only beyond this life, past death, that Dickinson knows she can find the answers to her most compelling questions. Her poems move less between the natural world and the self than between a projected view of the possibilities that lie beyond death and the frustrations of a consciousness confined to this world. The immortality Dickinson addresses is a condition that would allow her to see into a transcendent reality which would answer the questions no time on earth can ever resolve.

And yet, has not such an awareness of death informed the motives of the Romantics as well? What separates Dickinson's visions from theirs is the extent to which she dismisses the external world and her refusal to accept their consolations. Consequently her absorption in immortality, what she once called her "Flood subject," is more intense than theirs. Abjuring any verifiable notion of reality, Dickinson maintains that the only truth on which one can rely depends upon what one discovers by oneself. Living and dying thus assume the status of an experiment. This bias for experiment manifests itself formally in the riddles and definitions which are her poems—discreet attempts to define reality in terms of a single consciousness; hence the often contradictory and puzzling relation between poems which speak from opposing points of view. Taken together, Dickinson's poems are best read as a process, accounts of a continuing search for answers to questions that exceed the limits of even the most inquiring, active self.

Yet even the inquiring consciousness cannot be trusted completely, for Dickinson experiences an internal division which threatens her acquisitive powers. She asserts that she is alienated from a part of the mind which holds the energies of creativity, an estranged self who assumes, throughout the poems, a masculine identity. Not surprisingly, many of her poems become an attempt to reach this other self, to woo him to release the withheld power she needs in order to write. This struggle between consciousness and its antithet-

Afterword

ical yet essential adversary predominates as it replaces the Romantic desire for a wedding between the imagination and the world. That such an internal separation occurs reflects Dickinson's experience as a woman-poet; Adrienne Rich observes that,

"In writing at all—particularly an unorthodox and original poetry like Dickinson's—women have often felt in danger of losing their status as women. And this status has always been defined in terms of relationship to men—as daughter, sister, bride, wife, mother, mistress, Muse. Since the most powerful figures in patriarchal culture have been men, it seems natural that Dickinson would assign a masculine gender to that in herself which did not fit in with the conventional ideology of womanliness. To recognize and acknowledge our own interior power has always been a path mined with risks for women; to acknowledge that power and commit oneself to it as Emily Dickinson did was an immense decision."[1]

The Romantic ambition of bridging the distance between world and imagination fades before her desire to release the powers that hide within the estranged self. Because of the psychic turmoil that accompanies recognition of the "other's" presence, such inspiriting reunions can only intermittently capture the powers needed to write. Dialectical and ambivalent patterns between Dickinson and other poets, moreover, reflect this struggle occurring within the self as she seeks to unite powers at once necessary and destructive.

What most strongly determines Dickinson's sense of isolation, the need to subvert the Romantic vocabulary and refuse its consolations, depends upon her sense of self as "other." How could a woman without the faith that she too was a member of that great male company of poets, a woman living such an externally provincial existence, hope to vie with the powerful voices that awakened her imagination? Repeatedly her poems acknowledge the need for an-

---

[1] Adrienne Rich, "Vesuvius At Home: The Power of Emily Dickinson," *Parnassus: Poetry in Review* 5, no. 1 (Fall-Winter, 1976): 57.

Afterword

other presence to inform her own, yet she must banish *his* authority in order to assert *her* individual freedom. In this struggle toward self-definition, Dickinson turns to women writers, among them Elizabeth Barrett Browning, "Mrs. Lewes," as Dickinson was careful to call George Eliot, and her childhood friend, Helen Hunt Jackson. Her devotion to their work and what it symbolized—the burgeoning of a literary counter-tradition of women—implies this self-conscious ambition to create a poetry that would express her priorities. Indeed, Dickinson's experiments with language are more radical than those of her beloved Robert Browning or Tennyson, for her writing is informed not only by their questioning and skeptical imaginations, but by a deep sense of freedom, an inherent sense of discontinuity, which is the gift of the outsider.

Dickinson's most profound influence on subsequent poets cannot be fully or accurately measured until the middle of this century (in 1955) with the publication of Johnson's variorum edition. Since that time, a major reevaluation of Dickinson has begun, one which has led to our rediscovering a major poet, perhaps the most important, in nineteenth-century America. But even more significant is our growing recognition of Dickinson's awareness of the dominant male tradition, the canon formed by voices whose experiences she could only partially share. Educated within the Romantic tradition, Dickinson breaks from it in bold and original ways. Her deeply informed yet defiant gestures fulfill a crucial need for contemporary women poets. Adrienne Rich, Sylvia Plath, and (in a more oblique way) Elizabeth Bishop reveal the impact Dickinson's work continues to exercise. Her willingness to confront the male tradition, to win through and against it a deeply original voice—her refusal to be absorbed by or accept consolations not wholly her own—place Dickinson at the center of a newly emerging tradition of women poets. The risks she was willing to take depend upon an austere and powerful courage. Because of her daring, no woman poet need ever again feel so alone.

Selected Bibliography

BOOKS

Abrams, M. H. *The Mirror and the Lamp: Romantic Theory And The Critical Tradition.* New York: W. W. Norton & Co., 1958.

Anderson, Charles R. *Emily Dickinson's Poetry: Stairway of Surprise.* New York: Holt, Rinehart and Winston, 1960.

Anderson, Quentin. *The Imperial Self: An Essay in American Literary and Cultural History.* New York: Vintage Books, 1971.

Baker, Carlos. *Shelley's Major Poetry: The Fabric of A Vision.* New York: Russell & Russell, 1961.

Bate, Walter Jackson. *John Keats.* New York: Oxford University Press, 1966.

―――. *The Burden of the Past and the English Poet.* Cambridge: The Belknap Press of Harvard University Press, 1970.

―――, ed. *Keats: A Collection of Critical Essays.* Englewood Cliffs, New Jersey: Prentice-Hall, 1964.

Bianchi, Martha Gilbert. *Emily Dickinson Face to Face.* Hamden, Connecticut: Archon Books, 1932.

Bingham, Millicent Todd. *Emily Dickinson's Home: Letters of Edward Dickinson and His Family.* New York: Harper & Brothers Publishers, 1955.

Blake, C. R., and Carlton F. Wells. *The Recognition of Emily Dickinson: Selected Criticism Since 1890.* Ann Arbor: University of Michigan Press, 1964.

Bloom, Harold. *Romanticism and Consciousness: Essays in Criticism.* New York: W. W. Norton & Co., Inc., 1970.

―――. *Shelley's Mythmaking.* Ithaca, New York: Cornell University Press, 1969.

―――. *The Anxiety of Influence: A Theory of Poetry.* New York: Oxford University Press, 1973.

―――. *The Visionary Company: A Reading of English Romantic*

Selected Bibliography

Poetry. Garden City, New York: Anchor Books, Doubleday & Company, 1961.

———. *Yeats*. New York: Oxford University Press, 1970.

Brisman, Leslie. *Romantic Origins*. Ithaca and London: Cornell University Press, 1978.

Browning, Elizabeth Barrett. *Diary of E. B. B., 1831-1832*, ed. Philip Kelley and Ronald Hudson. Athens: Ohio University Press, 1969.

———. *The Complete Poetical Works*. Boston: Houghton Mifflin Company, 1900.

Browning, Robert. *Poetical Works*. London: Oxford University Press, 1967.

Buckingham, Willis J. *Emily Dickinson: An Annotated Bibliography: Writings, Scholarship, Criticism, and Ana, 1850-1968*. Bloomington: Indiana University Press, 1970.

Bush, Douglas. *John Keats: His Life and Writings*. New York: The Macmillan Co., 1966.

———. *Mythology and The Romantic Tradition in English Poetry*. New York: Norton, 1963.

———. *Selected Poems and Letters of John Keats*. Boston: Houghton Mifflin Company, 1959.

Byron, George Gordon. *The Complete Poems*. Cambridge: The Riverside Press, 1905.

Cameron, Sharon. *Lyric Time: Dickinson And The Limits of Genre*. Baltimore and London: The Johns Hopkins University Press, 1979.

Campbell, Joseph. *The Hero with a Thousand Faces*. Cleveland: World Publishing Co., 1949.

Capps, Jack L. *Emily Dickinson's Reading, 1836-1886*. Cambridge: Harvard University Press, 1966.

Chase, Richard. *Emily Dickinson*. New York: Wm. Sloane, 1951.

Cody, John. *After Great Pain: The Inner Life of Emily Dickinson*. Cambridge: Harvard University Press, 1971.

Coleridge, Samuel Taylor. *Biographia Literaria,* ed. with his aesthetical essays by J. Shawcross. 2 vols. London: Oxford at the Clarendon Press, 1907.

———. *The Poems*. London: Oxford University Press, 1927.

Selected Bibliography

Crews, Frederick, ed. *Psychoanalysis and Literary Process.* Cambridge, Massachusetts: Winthrop Publishers, 1970.
Dana, Charles A. *The Household Book of Poetry.* New York: Appleton and Company, 1860.
D'Avanzo, Mario L. *Keats's Metaphors for the Poetic Imagination.* Durham: Duke University Press, 1967.
Dickinson, Emily. *The Letters of Emily Dickinson,* ed. Thomas H. Johnson and Theodora Ward. Cambridge: Harvard University Press, 1958.
———. *The Poems of Emily Dickinson,* ed. Thomas H. Johnson. Cambridge: Harvard University Press, 1968.
Dickstein, Morris. *Keats and His Poetry: A Study in Development.* Chicago: University of Chicago Press, 1971.
Donoghue, Denis. *Emily Dickinson.* Minneapolis: The University of Minnesota Press, 1966.
Emerson, Ralph Waldo. *Selections from Ralph Waldo Emerson: An Organic Anthology,* ed. Stephen E. Whicher. Boston: Houghton Mifflin Company, 1960.
Evert, Walter. *Aesthetic and Myth in the Poetry of Keats.* Princeton: Princeton University Press, 1965.
Feidelson, Charles. *Symbolism and American Literature.* Chicago: The University of Chicago Press, 1966.
Ferguson, Frances. *Wordsworth: Language as Counter-Spirit.* New Haven and London: Yale University Press, 1977.
Fogle, Richard Harter. *The Imagery of Keats and Shelley: A Comparative Study.* Hamden, Connecticut: Archon Books, 1949.
Ford, Thomas W. *Heaven Beguiles The Tired: Death In The Poetry of Emily Dickinson.* University, Ala.: University of Alabama Press, 1966.
Frye, Northrop. *Fables of Identity: Studies in Poetic Mythology.* New York: Harcourt, Brace & World, Inc., 1963.
Gelpi, Albert J. *Emily Dickinson: The Mind of The Poet.* Cambridge: Harvard University Press, 1966.
———. *The Tenth Muse.* Cambridge: Harvard University Press, 1975.
Gide, André. *The Counterfeiters.* New York: Random House, Inc., 1955.

Selected Bibliography

Gilbert, Sandra M. and Susan Gubar. *The Madwoman in the Attic: The Woman Writer and the Nineteenth-Century Literary Imagination*, New Haven: Yale University Press, 1979.

Gittings, Robert. *John Keats: The Living Year*. Cambridge: Harvard University Press, 1954.

Goldberg, M. A. *The Poetics of Romanticism: Toward a Reading of John Keats*. Yellow Springs, Ohio: The Antioch Press, 1969.

Graves, Robert. *On Poetry: Collected Talks and Essays*. New York: Doubleday & Company, 1969.

Griffith, Clark. *The Long Shadow: Emily Dickinson's Tragic Poetry*. Princeton: Princeton University Press, 1964.

Hartman, Geoffrey H. *Beyond Formalism: Literary Essays 1958-1970*. New Haven and London: Yale University Press, 1970.

———. *The Unmediated Vision: An Interpretation of Wordsworth, Hopkins, Rilke, and Valery*. New York: Harcourt, Brace & World, Inc., 1966.

———. *Wordsworth's Poetry: 1787-1814*. New Haven and London: Yale University Press, 1964.

———, ed. *New Perspectives on Coleridge and Wordsworth: Selected Papers from the English Institute*. New York: Columbia University Press, 1972.

Hayter, Alethea. *Mrs. Browning: A Poet's Work and Its Setting*. London: Faber & Faber, 1962.

Hilles, Frederick W., and Harold Bloom, eds. *From Sensibility to Romanticism*. New York: Oxford University Press, 1965.

Jack, Ian. *Keats and the Mirror of Art*. Oxford: Clarendon Press, 1967.

Johnson, Thomas H. *Emily Dickinson: An Interpretive Biography*. Cambridge: Harvard University Press, 1964.

Jung, C. G. *Psychological Reflections*, ed. Jolande Jacobi. New York: Harper and Row, 1961.

Keats, John. *The Letters of John Keats*, ed. Hyder Edward Rollins. Cambridge: Harvard University Press, 1958.

———. *The Poems of John Keats*, ed. H. W. Garrod. London: Oxford University Press, 1966.

Selected Bibliography

———. *The Poetical Works of John Keats with a Life*, ed. James Russell Lowell. Boston: Little, Brown and Company, 1859.

———. *The Poetical Works of John Keats* (Complete in One Volume). New York: George P. Putnam, 1850.

Keller, Karl. *The Only Kangaroo Among the Beauty: Emily Dickinson and America*. Baltimore and London: The Johns Hopkins University Press, 1979.

Kher, Inder Nath. *The Landscape of Absence: Emily Dickinson's Poetry*. New Haven and London: Yale University Press, 1974.

Knight, G. Wilson. *Neglected Powers: Essays on Nineteenth and Twentieth Century Literature*. New York: Barnes & Noble, 1971.

Leyda, Jay. *The Years and Hours of Emily Dickinson*. New Haven: Yale University Press, 1960.

Lindberg-Seyersted, Brita. *The Voice of the Poet: Aspects of Style in the Poetry of Emily Dickinson*. Cambridge: Harvard University Press, 1968.

Lowell, James Russell. *Among My Books: Second Series*. Boston: Houghton Mifflin and Company, 1876.

Lubbers, Klaus. *Emily Dickinson: The Critical Revolution*. Ann Arbor: University of Michigan Press, 1968.

Lucas, Dolores Dyer. *Emily Dickinson and Riddle*. DeKalb: Northern Illinois Press, 1969.

Mack, Arien, ed. *Death in American Experience*. New York: Schocken Books, 1973.

MacLeish, Archibald, Louise Bogan, and Richard Wilbur. *Emily Dickinson: Three Views*. Amherst: Amherst College Press, 1960.

Melville, Herman. *Pierre; Or, The Ambiguities*. New York: Harper, 1852.

Merivale, Patricia. *Pan the Goat-God: His Myth in Modern Times*. Cambridge: Harvard University Press, 1969.

Miller, Betty. *Robert Browning: A Portrait*. London, 1952.

Miller, Ruth. *The Poetry of Emily Dickinson*. Middletown: Wesleyan University Press, 1968.

Milnes, Richard Monckton. *Life, Letters, and Literary Remains of John Keats*. New York: George P. Putnam, 1848.

Selected Bibliography

Moers, Ellen. *Literary Women*. New York: Anchor Press, 1977.

Moore, Thomas. *Letters and Journals of Lord Byron: With Notices of His Life*. New York: Harper, 1830.

Mudge, Jean McClure. *Emily Dickinson & the Image of Home*. Amherst: The University of Massachusetts Press, 1975.

Packer, Lona Mosk. *Christina Rossetti*. Berkeley: University of California Press, 1963.

Pearce, Roy Harvey. *The Continuity of American Poetry*. Princeton: Princeton University Press, 1961.

Perkins, David. *The Quest for Permanence: The Symbolism of Wordsworth, Shelley, and Keats*. Cambridge: Harvard University Press, 1959.

———. *Wordsworth and the Poetry of Sincerity*. Cambridge: Belknap Press of Harvard University Press, 1964.

Porter, David T. *The Art of Emily Dickinson's Early Poetry*. Great Britain: Oxford University Press, 1964.

Poulet, Julia. *Shelley in America in the Nineteenth Century: His Relation to American Critical Thought and Influence*. New York: Gordian Press, 1969.

Pulos, C. E. *The Deep Truth: A Study of Shelley's Scepticism*. Lincoln: University of Nebraska Press, 1954.

Radley, Virginia L. *Elizabeth Barrett Browning*. New York: Twayne Publishers, Inc., 1972.

Rieger, James. *The Mutiny Within: The Heresies of Percy Bysshe Shelley*. New York: George Braziller, 1967.

Rollins, Hyder Edward. *Keats' Reputation in America to 1848*. Cambridge: Harvard University Press, 1946.

Rosenbaum, S. P. *A Concordance to the Poems of Emily Dickinson*. Ithaca: Cornell University Press, 1966.

Rossetti, Christina Georgina. *The Poetical Works*. Hildensheim: Georg Olms Verlag, 1970.

Scribner's Monthly. Vol. II, November 1875-April 1876. New York: Scribner's & Co.

Sewall, Richard B. *The Life of Emily Dickinson*. Vols. I and II. New York: Farrar, Straus and Giroux, 1974.

———. *The Lyman Letters: New Light on Emily Dickinson and Her Family*. Amherst: The University of Massachusetts Press, 1965.

Selected Bibliography

———, ed. *Emily Dickinson: A Collection of Critical Essays.* Englewood Cliffs, New Jersey: Prentice-Hall, 1963.

Shelley, Percy Bysshe. *Poetical Works*, ed. Thomas Hutchinson. London: Oxford University Press, 1967.

Sherwood, William Robert. *Circumference and Circumstance: Stages in the Mind and Art of Emily Dickinson.* New York and London: Columbia University Press, 1968.

Shove, Fredegond. *Christina Rossetti: A Study.* Cambridge: At The University Press, 1972.

Stevens, Wallace. *The Collected Poems of Wallace Stevens.* New York: Alfred A. Knopf, 1968.

Taggard, Genevieve. *The Life and Mind of Emily Dickinson.* New York: Alfred A. Knopf, 1930.

Taplin, Gardner. *The Life of Elizabeth Barrett Browning.* New Haven: Yale University Press, 1931.

The Poetical Works of Coleridge, Shelley and Keats Complete in One Volume. Philadelphia: Thomas, Cowperthwait & Co., 1839.

Thomas, Eleanor Walter. *Christina Georgina Rossetti.* New York: Columbia University Press, 1931.

Thorpe, Clarence Dewitt. *The Mind of John Keats.* New York: Oxford University Press, 1936.

Todd, John Emerson. *Emily Dickinson's Use of the Persona.* The Hague: Mouton & Co., 1973.

Trelawny, Edward John. *Recollections of the Last Days of Shelley and Byron.* Boston: Tichnor and Fields, 1858.

Walsh, John Evangelist. *The Hidden Life of Emily Dickinson.* New York: Simon and Schuster, 1971.

Ward, Aileen. *John Keats: The Making of a Poet.* New York: The Viking Press, 1963.

Ward, Theodora. *The Capsule of the Mind: Chapters in the Mind of Emily Dickinson.* Cambridge: The Belknap Press of Harvard University Press, 1961.

Weisbuch, Robert. *Emily Dickinson's Poetry.* Chicago: The University of Chicago Press, 1975.

Weiskel, Thomas. *The Romantic Sublime: Studies in the Structure and Psychology of Transcendence.* Baltimore: Johns Hopkins University Press, 1971.

Winters, Yvor. *In Defense of Reason.* Denver: Alan Swallow, 1943.

SELECTED ARTICLES

Cambon, Glauco. "Emily Dickinson's Circumference." *Sewanee Review.* 84:342-50.

Cameron, Sharon. " 'A Loaded Gun': Dickinson and the Dialectic of Rage." *PMLA.* 93, iii:423-437.

Carton, Evan. "Dickinson and the Divine: The Terror of Integration, the Terror of Detachment." *ESQ,* Vol. 24, 4th Quarter 1978, pp. 242-252.

D'Avanzo, Mario. "Dickinson's 'The Reticent Volcano' and Emerson." *American Transcendental Quarterly.* 14:11-13.

———. "Emily Dickinson's and Emerson's 'Presentiment.' " *ESQ: A Journal of the American Renaissance.* 58:157-159.

———. " 'Unto the White Creator': The Snow of Dickinson and Emerson." *New England Quarterly.* 45:278-280.

Eitner, Walter H. "Emily Dickinson's Awareness of Whitman: A Reappraisal." *Walt Whitman Review.* 22:111-115.

Faber, M. D. "Psychoanalytic Remarks on a Poem by Emily Dickinson." *Psychoanalytic Review.* 56, ii:247-264.

Ford, Thomas W. "Thoreau's Cosmic Mosquito and Dickinson's Terrestrial Fly." *The New England Quarterly.* 48:487-504.

Gilbert, Sandra M. "Patriarchal Poetry and Women Readers: Reflections on Milton's Bogey." *PMLA.* 93, iii:368-382.

Hagenbüchle, Roland. "Precision and Indeterminacy in the Poetry of Emily Dickinson." *ESQ: A Journal of the American Renaissance.* 74:33-56.

Harper's New Monthly Magazine. Vol. II, September 1851.

Juhasz, Suzanne. " 'A Privilege So Awful': Emily Dickinson as Woman Poet." *San Jose Studies.* 2, ii:94-107.

McIntosh, James. "Emerson's Unmoored Self." *The Yale Review,* LXV:232-240.

Pollak, Vivian R. "Emily Dickinson's Literary Allusions." *Essays in Literature.* Western Illinois University. 1:54-68.

Porter, David. "The Crucial Experience in Emily Dickinson's Poetry." *ESQ: A Journal of the American Renaissance.* 20, iv:280-290.

Selected Bibliography

———. "Emily Dickinson: The Poetics of Doubt." *ESQ: A Journal of the American Renaissance*. 60:86-93.
Rich, Adrienne. "Vesuvius at Home: The Power of Emily Dickinson," *Parnassus: Poetry in Review*. 5, i:49-74.
Richmond, Lee J. "Emersonian Echos in Dickinson's 'These are the Signs.'" *American Transcendentalist Quarterly*. 29:2-3.
Scribner's Monthly. Vol. II, November 1875 to April 1876. New York: Scribner's & Co.
Stewart, Garrett. "*Lamia* and the Language of Metamorphosis." *Studies in Romanticism*. 15, i:3-41.
The Atlantic Monthly. Vols. I-XXXIV. 1857-1874.
Vendler, Helen. "The Experiential Beginnings of Keats's Odes," *Studies in Romanticism*, Vol. II, Summer 1973. The Graduate School, Boston University.
Wilner, Eleanor. "The Poetics of Emily Dickinson." *ELH: Journal of English Literary History*. 38:126-154.
Yetman, Michael G. "Emily Dickinson and the English Tradition." *Texas Studies in Literature and Language*. XV, i:129-147.
Yoder, R. A. "Toward the 'Titmouse Dimension': The Development of Emerson's Poetic Style." *PMLA*. 87:255-270.

INDEX

Abrams, M. H., 10, 50n
abyss, 179, 180; and heaven, 180; Edwards' blazing pit, 181; internalization of, 182; literary sources of, 182n
Anderson, Charles, 6, 6n, 45n, 91n, 93n, 109n, 151n
Apollo, 70, 85
Apuleius, 72
Arachne, 161, 182
Archaeologica Graeca, 111-12
astronomical absorption, images of, 145-50; and the identity of the self, 151-52; as threat and redemption, 153
Atlantic Monthly, 113
Augustine of Hippo, 169

Bailey, Benjamin, 75
Bate, Walter Jackson, *The Burden of the Past and the English Poet*, 82, 111n, 112n
Bible, 4n, 6, 20; Genesis, 23; John, 53
Bishop, Elizabeth, 186
Blake, William, 15, 16
Bloom, Harold, 8-9, 13-14, 83n, 88, 122n, 134n, 135
Boehme, Jakob, 182
Bogan, Louise, 4n
Bowdoin, Elbridge G., 17
Brazil, as ultimate exotic, 167
Browning, Elizabeth Barrett, 15, 27, 186; *works discussed: Aurora Leigh*, 29, 114n; "A Musical Instrument," 29-31; *Sonnets from the Portuguese*, 29
Browning, Robert, 7, 186
Burke, Edmund, 60
Burnet, Thomas, 182

Bush, Douglas, 72n-73n, 75
Byron, George Gordon, Lord, 9-10, 101, 130

Calvinist, 5; consciousness, 16; Dickinson's fear of, 67; concept of Grace, 91; vision of Hell, 181n
Cambon, Glauco, 161n, 172n-73n
Cameron, Sharon, 4n-5n
Campbell, Joseph, 31
Carton, Evan, 164
centre, 56; *see* circumference
Chambers, Robert, 113n
Christ, 27, 111, 125, 153, 156
circumference, 16, 138-39, 144, 166; Wordsworthian, 56; *see* "centre"
Cody, John, 100, 132
Coleridge, Samuel Taylor, 9-10; *Frost at Midnight* and ED's "The Frost Was Never Seen," 10, 51-54
compensation, 165
consciousness, adversarial, 171, 175; relation to nature, 172; split, 173; *see* stranger
correspondence, 165; between self and nature, absent in ED, 165; *see* nature
Cupid, 72

Dana, Charles A., 113n
D'Avanzo, Mario, 76, 77, 112
death, 7, 16; temptation and fear of, 18; ED's poems as acts of defense against, 61-67 passim; as "great divorcer," 117-18; Keats's and ED's views of, 114-21, 147; Shelley's and ED's attitudes toward, 142; in "Behind Me—dips

197

Index

death (cont.)
  Eternity—," 152; ED's poems responding to silence of, 165-69; and ED's quest for immortality, 184
de Man, Paul, 122n
De Quincey, Thomas, 114n
Dickinson, Edward, 26n, 127n
Dickinson, Emily, and the Romantic tradition, 3-4 and passim; relationship to nativist sources, 5; and the critical treatment of, 4-8; a woman poet, 7 and passim; as American Romantic, 8 and passim; her strategies of subversion, 9 and passim
Dickinson's letters, 16, 23, 24, 25, 39, 58, 95, 98, 99, 100, 104, 107, 121, 153, 174, 179
Dickinson, Susan Gilbert, 15n, 137
Dickstein, Morris, 115n

Edwards, Jonathan, 181-82
Eliot, George [Mrs. Lewes], 186
Emerson, Ralph Waldo, 5, 6, 9-11, 34, 133, 161-82 passim, 183; *works discussed*: "The Poet," 162, 164; "Experience," 162-63, 171; "Illusions," 163; "Ode to Beauty," 163-64; "Nature," 164, 171; "Circles," 164, 166, 169-70; "Spiritual Laws," 173; "Fate," 176, 177-79; *works cited*: "The Divinity School Address," 170; "Merlin," 172; "The American Scholar," 172, 177
epitaph, poem as funeral monument, 64-65
Etna, 176

Ferguson, Frances, 64n
French, Daniel Chester, 138
Freud, Sigmund, 13n-14n
Frye, Northrop, 61n-62n

Gelpi, Albert, 4, 4n, 43-44, 89, 93n-94n
gender identity, and the woman poet, 9; and language, 12, 185
Gilbert, Sandra, 7n, 9-10, 131n
Gittings, Robert, 70
God, as *deus absconditus*, 27; in competition with lover/muse/poet, 27
Griffith, Clark, 16
Gubar, Susan, 9-10, 131n

Hagenbuchle, Roland, 4n, 122n-23n
Hartman, Geoffrey, 34, 35, 37-38, 44-45, 48-49, 50, 118, 182n
Harvard, John, 138
Haydon, Benjamin R., 101
Hazlitt, William, 114n
Higginson, Thomas Wentworth, 23n, 39, 99, 113n, 153
Holland, Mrs. Josiah Gilbert, 23
Homans, Margaret, 12n
Horace, 62-63
Hunt, Leigh, 114

imagination, Wordsworthian, 40 and 34-67 passim; and the natural world, 34-67 passim, 185; and ED's internal landscape, 42; and time in ED's poetry, 74; and internalization of nature in Shelley and ED, 122-23; and astronomical images of in Shelley and ED, 129-30; *see* nature
inscription, process of, 44; ED's transformation of, 44; Romantic nature-inscriptions, 44; the genre in England, 44

Jackson, Helen Hunt, 113n, 186
Jacob, 23
Johnson, Thomas H., 15, 39n-40n, 139n, 186

Index

Kabbalah, 13
Keats, John, 3, 9, 134n, 183; and Dickinson, 68-121; and the erotic trope for poetic creation, 68; and the eternal female, 70 (*see* stranger); *poems discussed*: "To Ailsa Rock," 69; "Read me a lesson, Muse, and speak it loud," 69; *The Fall of Hyperion: A Fragment*, 70, 116-17; "Ode to Psyche," 71-76; *Endymion*, 77, 80n, 97n, 103; "To J. H. Reynolds Esqu.," 87; "Ode On A Grecian Urn," 93-94; "On the Grasshopper and the Cricket," compared to ED's "Further in Summer than the Birds—," 96-98; *letters*: 75, 76, 82, 85, 92, 95, 100, 101, 102, 106, 111, 112, 116; *works cited: La Belle Dame Sans Merci*, 69, 71, 75; *Lamia*, 69; *Hyperion*, 70; *Ode to a Nightingale*, 88, 115, 119-21; "Isabella; Or, the Pot of Basil," 103; Ode on Melancholy, 103; "Ode to Apollo," 103; "On Sitting Down To Read King Lear Once Again," 107; "God of The Meridian," 107; "Sleep and Poetry," 108; *Hyperion*, 108-09; "To —," ("What can I do to drive away"), 109
Keller, Karl, 5

Leyda, Jay, 107, 116n
lightning, Dickinson's characterization of, 125-31; Webster's definition of, 127; Emerson's image for power, 176; *see* volcanoes
Longfellow, Henry Wadsworth, 138
Lord, Otis P., 95
love, and poetic election, 126-27
lover-goddess, Keats's image of, 115
Lowell, James Russell, 114, 115n

Lyman, Joseph, 105
lyric, as dramatic form, 9; "Greater Romantic," 10, 50; Dickinson's subversion of, 50-54; ED's "The Frost was never seen—" as formal subversion of Coleridge's *Frost at Midnight*, 50-54

MacLeish, Archibald, 4
male poet, and his maieutic impulse, 19
master poet, and masculine identity, 26
McIntosh, James, 173
Melville, Herman, 34
Memnon stone, as symbol of Dickinson's poetic adversary and muse, 66; see muse
Merivale, Patricia, 29-30
Miller, J. Hillis, 124
Milton(ic), 6, 20-21, 41, 83, 170n; post-, 7n
Minerva, 161
Moers, Ellen, 15
Murry, John Middleton, 75
muse, 3, 20-21, 32, 185; ED's sense of contrasted to Romantics' conception, 18-19; as male Composite Precursor, 19; male poet's relation to contrasted to ED's, 27; ED's compared to Keats's *femme*, 82

nature, self's relation to, 7; ED's distrust of, 17; relation of man to nature, 34-35 and 34-67 passim; and the imagination, 42, 161-81; rhetorical role of, 42-43; Wordsworth's vision of compared to ED's, 44; comparison of Keats's and ED's views of, 85; ED's conversion of, 134; images of internal events, 160; poet as reader of (Emerson and ED), 162-64; as allegorical projection of self, 165;

199

Index

nature (cont.)
as mystery, 179; as untrustworthy, 183
negative capability, in Keats and ED, 99–103
negative way, Keats's conception compared to ED's, 80–82
Nietzsche, Friedrich, 13, 161
Niles, Thomas, 98
Norcross, Louise and Frances, 24, 26n

oral deprivation, in Keats and Dickinson, 104–05

Pan, 29–31; Wordsworthian, 30
patriarchal, canon, 7; the tradition, 7; the tradition and women poets, 11
Paul, Sherman, 165n
Pearce, Roy Harvey, 10, 10n
Perkins, David, 112, 115
Petrarch and Laura, 108
Plath, Sylvia, 186
poet, as language-maker, 10; as hero, 21; and metaphor of the quest, 21; and role of woman, 21; as reader of nature, 164–65, 169; Emerson's conception of, 170; Saadi as Emersonian, 174
poetic influence, 9; and gender identity, 11; and patriarchal tradition, 11; the Oedipal struggle, 13; dilemma of, 18–19; process for Victorian female poets, 27–31 passim; between Shelley and ED, 144–45
Pollack, Vivian R., 6n
post-Enlightenment, 3, 21
Power, Julia, 133n–34n
precursor, composite male figure, 15; and the muse, 18–19, 32; Keats's and ED's attitudes toward, 82–83
Prometheanism, in Shelley and ED, 153; sacrificial quality of, 155–58
Psyche, 72
Pulos, C. E., 140

repression, Freud on, 22
Rich, Adrienne, 4n, 131, 185
Romanticism, 3–4, 7 passim; American, 8; naturalizing, 9–10, 183; lyric, 9; ED's relation to, 161, 183, 184–86; consolations of, 184
Rossetti, Christina, 15, 27; and the problem of creativity, 28; rhetoric of disguise, 28; *works discussed*: "Goblin Market," 28; "The Dead City," 28n; "My Dream," 28n; "Winter: My Secret," 28; and repression, 28–32; and renunciation, 31

self, 7; Emerson's responsibility for, 22; split, 26, 179; Emerson's concept of, 173; ED's transformation of Emersonian, 173; "other" as masculine, 173; ED's compared to Emersonian and Whitmanian forms, 175; power emanating from, 176; in relation to the Over-Soul, 179; giantism of, 181; precariousness of, 181; sovereignty of, 183–85
Severn, Joseph, 113
Sewall, Richard B., 5, 5n, 105n, 138
Shakespeare, William, 4n, 105n
Shelley, Percy Bysshe, 3, 9, 112, 183, 123–60; and ED's conception of poetic word, 122; image of lightning in, 130; volcanoes in, 131–33;
    works discussed: "The Triumph of Life," 129, 152–53, 154n; *Epipsychidion*, 130, 135–36, 137. 139–51 passim; *Prometheus Un-*

200

Index

bound, 131, 153, 154-55, 158; "Ode to the West Wind," 138, 157-58
 works cited: "Adonais," 130; *The Mask of Anarchy*, 132; "Liberty," 132; "Marianne's Dream," 132; "Orpheus," 135; "The Cenci," 135; "To Edward Williams," 135; "Goodnight," 137; "Mutability," 137; "On a Faded Violet," 137; "Lines written among the Euganean Hills," 137, 159; "The Past," 137; "To the Moon," 137; "On a Faded Violet," 137; "The Sensitive Plant," 137; "The Cloud," 137; "To A Skylark," 137; "The Waning Moon," 138; "Ode to Liberty," 138
skepticism, ED's, 183
Spenser, Edmund, 76
spider, 92-93; Arachnean form, 161
Stevens, Wallace, 68, 120n
Stewart, Garrett, 71n
stranger, 19; and the libido, 22; and preceptor, 24; Coleridge's, 52; and Keats's eternal female, 70; as erotic other, 77; as consciousness, 173; sexualized other, 173
subversion, ED's strategies of, 9
Swedenborg, Emanuel, 13

Tennyson, Alfred Lord, 7, 186
Thomas, Eleanor Walter, 15

Van Gogh, Vincent, 130
Vendler, Helen, 94
Vesuvius, 131, 176
Vico, Giovanni Battista, 13
Virgil, 182n
volcanoes, in Shelley, ED, and Emerson, 131-33; Etna, Vesuvius, 176; ED's identification of 177; oral potency and poetry, 177; *see* lightning

Walsh, John Evangelist, 8n
Ward, Aileen, 103
Ward, Theodora, 16
Warren, Austin, 6, 6n
Wasserman, Earl R., 134n
Webster, Noah, 127
Weisbuch, Robert, 4n, 10, 10n-11n, 57n, 122n-23n
Wesley, Charles, 34
Wesling, Donald, 59-60
Wilbur, Richard, 4
Whicher, George Frisbie, 5n
Whicher, Stephen, 175
Whitman, Walt, 122, 175
Winters, Yvor, 5, 83, 84n-85n, 97n
women poets, 3, 7, 11, 31, 186; and the male-dominated tradition, 14; counter-tradition of, 15; and the role of muse, 21
Woodhouse, Richard, 100
word, 3-4; the Holy and the poetic, 6; enchant and infect, 18; ED's figural modes of language, 124; transubstantiation of, 124-25
Wordsworth, William, 3, 9, 18, 34-67 passim, 83; on the poet's relation to nature, 35; *works discussed*: *The Prelude*, 35, 36, 41; "Preface," *Lyrical Ballads*, 36; "Evening Voluntary 1X," 36; "Intimations Ode," 37; "Preface to the Edition of 1814," *The Excursion*, 40; "Guilt and Sorrows Or Incidents Upon Salisbury Plain," 49-50; *The Excursion*, Bk. IV, 54-55; "Written With A Slate Pencil On A Stone, On The Side of The Mountain of Black Comb," 55-56; "Elegiac Stanzas, suggested by a Picture of Peele Castle . . . ," 58-60

Yeats, William Butler, 13
Yetman, Michael G., 4n
Yoder, R. A., 11n, 174

LIST OF DICKINSON POEMS

(Poems Discussed)

The Frost was never seen—(1202), 10, 51-54
I think I was enchanted (593), 15n
The life doth prove the precept, who obey shall happy be, (1), 17
Come slowly—Eden! (2]]), 17-18
We shun it ere it comes, (1580), 19
I would not paint—a picture—(505), 19-20
Growth of Man—like Growth of Nature—(750), 21
My Soul—accused me—And I quailed—(753), 22
I reckon—when I count at all—(569), 22
A little East of Jordan, (59), 23, 38-39, 113n
Give little Anguish—(310), 25
I am afraid to own a Body—(1090), 25
Of Consciousness, her awful Mate (894), 26
Art thou the thing I wanted? (1282), 27
Tried always and Condemned by thee (1559), 32
He was my host—he was my guest, (1721), 33
The Spirit is the Conscious Ear. (733), 43
Growth of Man—like Growth of Nature—(750), 43
I've dropped my Brain—My Soul is numb—(1046), 45-46
If I shouldn't be alive (182), 47
After great pain, a formal feeling comes—(341), 47

The name—of it—is "Autumn"—(656), 48
There's a certain Slant of light, (258), 54-55
His mind of man a secret makes (1663), 56n-57n
Must be a Wo—(571), 57-58
When I hoped I feared—(1181), 59
I can wade Grief—(252), 60
It dropped so low—in my Regard—(747), 60-61
After a hundred years (1147), 61-62
An honest Tear (1192), 62-63
She laid her docile Crescent down (1396), 63-64
This was a Poet—It is That (448), 64-65
Put up my lute! (261), 66-67
This is a Blossom of the Brain—(945), 73
Myself was formed—a Carpenter—(488), 73-74
All that I do (1496), 77-78
To pile like Thunder to its close (1247), 78-79, 126 ff.
We dream—it is good we are dreaming—(531), 79-81
I rose—because He sank—(616), 81-82
The Props assist the House (1142), 84
Bloom—is Result—to meet a Flower (1058), 86
The Flower must not blame the Bee—(206), 86
Did the Harebell loose her girdle (213), 86-87

Index

There is another sky, (2), 89-90

There is a Zone whose even Years (1056), 90

I reckon—when I count at all—(569), 90-91

A spider sewed at Night (1138), 92-93

The Spider as an Artist (1275), 93

Dominion lasts until obtained—(1257), 94-95

How much the present moment means (1380), 95-96

Further in Summer than the Birds (1068), 97-98

As imperceptibly as Grief (1540), 98-99

To learn the Transport by the Pain—(167), 101-02

I shall know why—when Time is over—(193), 102-03

I had been hungry, all the Years—(579), 104-05

He ate and drank the precious Words—(1587), 105-06

Art thou the thing I wanted? (1282), 105n-06n

My Cocoon tightens—Colors teaze—(1099), 106

Bind me—I still can sing—(1005), 110

I'm ceded—I've stopped being Their's—(508), 110-11

Here, where the Daisies fit my Head (1037), 111n

Exhilaration—is within—(383), 112-13

If your Nerve, deny you—(292), 114-15

Of all the Souls that stand create—(664), 116

It was not Death, for I stood up, (510), 117-18

Those who have been in the Grave the longest—(922), 118-19

Silence is all we dread (1251), 119

Beauty crowds me till I die (1654), 120

I died for Beauty—but was scarce (449), 120-21

A Word made Flesh is seldom (1651), 124-25

You'll know it—as you know 'tis Noon—(420), 126

It struck me—every Day—(362), 126

To pile like Thunder to it's close (1247), 126-27

I would not paint—a picture—(505), 127

The Soul's distinct connection (974), 128

Tell all the Truth but tell it slant—(1129), 128-29

The Lightning is a yellow Fork (1173), 129

I have never seen "Volcanoes"—(175), 132-133

My Life had stood—a Loaded Gun—(754), 133

A still—Volcano—Life—(601), 133

This Consciousness that is aware (822), 134-35

A *Wounded* Deer—leaps highest—(165), 135

This Merit hath the worst—(979), 136

Good to hide, and hear 'em hunt! (842), 136

Circumference, thou Bride (1620), 138-40

Till Death—is narrow Loving—(907), 141-43

Arrows enamored of his Heart—(1629), 143

The Admirations—and Contempts—of time—(906), 148

In thy long Paradise of Light (1145), 148

We met as Sparks—Diverging Flints (958), 149

Index

The pattern of the sun (1550), 149-50

I make His Crescent fill or lack—(909), 150

Behind Me—dips Eternity—(721), 151-53

The smouldering embers blush—(1132), 153-54

Sang from the Heart, Sire, (1059), 155-58

The wind drew off (1694), 158-59

Sweet Skepticism of the Heart—(1413), 164

The Tint I cannot take—is best—(627), 166-67

I asked no other thing—(621), 167-68

Those—dying then, (1551), 168

Still own thee—still thou art (1633), 168-69

The Soul unto itself (683), 175-76

When Etna basks and purrs (1146), 176-77

A still—Volcano—Life—(601), 177

Two swimmers wrestled on the spar—(201), 178

A Pit—but Heaven over it—(1712), 180

I stepped from Plank to Plank (875), 180-81

Library of Congress Cataloging in Publication Data

Diehl, Joanne Feit, 1947-
  Dickinson and the Romantic imagination.

  Bibliography: p.
  Includes index.
  1. Dickinson, Emily, 1830-1886—Criticism and interpretation. 2. Romanticism. 3. Influence (Literary, artistic, etc.) 4. Feminism and literature. I. Title.
PS1541.Z5D5   811'.4   81-47121
ISBN 0-691-06478-4   AACR2

Joanne Feit Diehl is in the Department of English, University of Texas, Austin.

GPSR Authorized Representative: Easy Access System Europe - Mustamäe tee 50, 10621 Tallinn, Estonia, gpsr.requests@easproject.com